Military History Chronicles

Also from Westphalia Press
westphaliapress.org

The Idea of the Digital University

Dialogue in the Roman-Greco World

The History of Photography

International or Local Ownership?: Security Sector Development in Post-Independent Kosovo

Lankes, His Woodcut Bookplates

Opportunity and Horatio Alger

The Role of Theory in Policy Analysis

The Little Confectioner

Non-Profit Organizations and Disaster

The Idea of Neoliberalism: The Emperor Has Threadbare Contemporary Clothes

Social Satire and the Modern Novel

Ukraine vs. Russia: Revolution, Democracy and War: Selected Articles and Blogs, 2010-2016

James Martineau and Rebuilding Theology

A Strategy for Implementing the Reconciliation Process

Issues in Maritime Cyber Security

A Different Dimension: Reflections on the History of Transpersonal Thought

Iran: Who Is Really In Charge?

Contracting, Logistics, Reverse Logistics: The Project, Program and Portfolio Approach

Unworkable Conservatism: Small Government, Freemarkets, and Impracticality

Springfield: The Novel

Lariats and Lassos

Ongoing Issues in Georgian Policy and Public Administration

Growing Inequality: Bridging Complex Systems, Population Health and Health Disparities

Designing, Adapting, Strategizing in Online Education

Pacific Hurtgen: The American Army in Northern Luzon, 1945

Natural Gas as an Instrument of Russian State Power

New Frontiers in Criminology

Feeding the Global South

Beijing Express: How to Understand New China

The Rise of the Book Plate: An Exemplative of the Art

MILITARY HISTORY CHRONICLES
VOLUME 2, NUMBER 2 • FALL 2025 CAMPAIGN

Westphalia Press
An imprint of Policy Studies Organization
1367 Connecticut Ave NW
Washington, D.C. 20036
info@ipsonet.org

ISBN: 978-1-63723-691-8

Cover and interior design by Jeffrey Barnes
jbarnesbook.design

Daniel Gutierrez-Sandoval, Executive Director
PSO and Westphalia Press

Updated material and comments on this edition
can be found at the Westphalia Press website:
www.westphaliapress.org

MILITARY HISTORY CHRONICLES

Volume 2, Number 2 • Fall 2025

Jeffrey Ballard, Editor-in-Chief

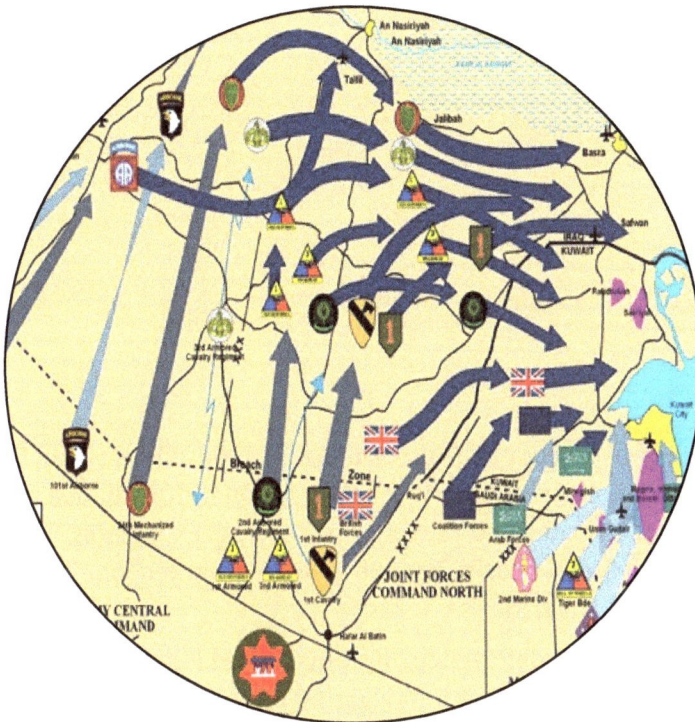

Westphalia Press

An imprint of Policy Studies Organization

On the cover: Thirty-five years ago, on August 7, 1990, **Operation Desert Shield** was launched as the international response to Iraq's invasion of Kuwait just days earlier. Its mission was to defend Saudi Arabia and prevent further Iraqi expansion. This strategic buildup of U.S. and coalition forces—nearly 700,000 troops—marked one of the largest military mobilizations since World War II.

Desert Shield was a display of deterrence, diplomacy, and logistical coordination. Coalition nations united under a common goal, navigating cultural sensitivities and political complexities, especially with Western troops stationed in Saudi Arabia. The operation wasn't combat—it was preparation. It bought time, built alliances, and sent a clear message to Saddam Hussein: aggression would not go unanswered.

The United Nations issued resolutions demanding Iraq's withdrawal, culminating in a deadline of January 15, 1991. When Hussein refused, Desert Shield transitioned into **Operation Desert Storm**—the combat phase—on January 17.

Though quieter than the dramatic airstrikes that followed, Desert Shield was crucial. It restored American confidence in its military, showcased technological advances, and demonstrated the power of global unity. It was the sentinel that held the line, the calm before the storm, and the foundation for victory.

Military History Chronicles
Volume 2, Number 2 • Fall 2025
© 2025 Policy Studies Organization

TABLE OF CONTENTS

Dispatch No. 4 1
Jeffrey Ballard

Towards a Reassessment of Livy as Military Historian: Some
Preliminary Findings 3
Seth Kendall

The Red Stick War 1813–1814 19
Dr. Matt Meador

Manolis Bandouvas and the Interplay of Tradition, Resistance,
and Allied Strategy in Crete During World War II 45
Emmanouil Peponas

Between Two Worlds: Mattis, Conviction, and Politics in
the Fallujah Ceasefire 67
Mason Krebsbach

Book Review: Andrew Eric Wright Sr.'s *Death Before Dismount:
U.S. Army Tanks in Iraq* 83
Dr. Robert Young

Book Review: Peter Harmsen's *Bernhard Sindberg: The Schindler
of Nanjing* 87
Aisha Manus

Book Review: Douglas Brunt's *The Mysterious Case of Rudolf Diesel:
Genius, Power, and Deception on the Eve of World War 1* 91
Clayton Willis

Battlefield Tour: Gettysburg: A Look at A Great American Battlefield 95
Joseph Terry

Call for Papers 109

Dispatch No. 4

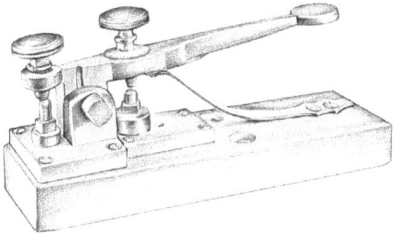

At *Military History Chronicles*, our commitment to preserving the full, unvarnished record of the past is not just a mission—it is a responsibility. We believe military history must be told with clarity, courage, and respect for complexity, even when it unsettles or challenges prevailing narratives.

In March, the American Historical Association and the Organization of American Historians issued a joint statement condemning recent efforts to censor historical content across federal websites, public museums, and other government resources. We fully agree with this position.

As a matter of principle, *Military History Chronicles* will no longer maintain a presence on any Meta-owned social media platform. We cannot in good conscience support any outlet that facilitates the distortion, erasure, or sanitization of critical chapters of human history.

This troubling trend of institutional censorship—whether by omission, simplification, or suppression—only deepens our resolve. We reaffirm our dedication to fostering critical inquiry, amplifying primary sources, and engaging honestly with the past.

We encourage our readers to access our work directly at www.militaryhistorychronicles.org, where our complete archive remains freely available and editorially independent.

Thank you for standing with us in defense of historical truth.

Jeff Ballard

Editor-in-Chief
Honiara, Guadalcanal
Solomon Islands
July 17, 2025

doi: 10.18278/mhc.2.2.1

Towards a Reassessment of Livy as Military Historian: Some Preliminary Findings

Seth Kendall

Associate Professor of History
Georgia Gwinnett College

Abstract

Contemporary evaluations of Titus Livius's qualities as a historian highlight the numerous deficiencies perceived in his works. One of the most profound is Livy's weakness in discussing military matters. However, given the enormous importance of Livy's work for understanding Roman history and the importance of war in the text itself, a more detailed analysis of how he handles military affairs seems warranted.

This essay will provide such an analysis. Due to the vastness of Livy's work, it will not attempt to discuss the whole of it; rather, it will restrict itself to exploring how war and combat are handled in Livy's first pentad (Books 1-5). It will describe how Livy tends to present military operations, to test the assertion that (as one critic points out) Livy's battle pieces "do not reveal just what [modern military historians might] want to know."

Keywords: Livy, Roman History, Ancient Warfare, Roman Warfare, *pilum*

Hacia una reevaluación de Tito Livio como historiador militar: Algunos hallazgos preliminares

Resumen

Las evaluaciones contemporáneas de las cualidades de Tito Livio como historiador ponen de relieve las numerosas deficiencias percibidas en su obra. Una de las más profundas es su debilidad al abordar cuestiones militares. Sin embargo, dada la enorme importancia de la obra de Tito Livio para comprender la historia romana y la importancia de la guerra en el propio texto, parece justificado un análisis más detallado de su tratamiento de los asuntos militares.

Este ensayo ofrecerá dicho análisis. Debido a la vastedad de la obra de Tito Livio, no se intentará analizarla en su totalidad; más bien,

doi: 10.18278/mhc.2.2.2

se limitará a explorar cómo se abordan la guerra y el combate en los primeros cinco libros de Livio. Se describirá cómo Tito Livio suele presentar las operaciones militares, para comprobar la afirmación de que (como señala un crítico) sus piezas de batalla «no revelan precisamente lo que [los historiadores militares modernos] podrían querer saber».

Palabras clave: Tito Livio, Historia romana, Guerra antigua, Guerra romana, pilum

重新评价作为军事史学家的李维——一些初步发现

摘要

关于提图斯·李维作为历史学家的当代评价强调了其作品中的诸多不足之处。其中最突出的不足之处是李维在讨论军事问题上的不足。然而，鉴于李维的作品对于理解罗马史的巨大意义，以及战争在文本中的重要性，似乎有必要对他如何处理军事事务一事进行更详细的分析。

本文将提供这样的分析。由于李维作品之多，本文不会试图讨论其全部内容；相反，本文将仅限于探讨李维在前五部书（第一至第五部）中如何处理战争和战斗。本文将描述李维倾向于如何呈现军事行动，以验证正如一位评论家所指出的断言，即李维的战争作品"并未揭示（现代军事史学家）可能想知道的内容"。

关键词：李维，罗马史，古代战争，罗马战争，皮卢姆重标枪

I. Livy the Military Historian: Modern Appraisals

All modern students of Roman history will readily acknowledge the enormous importance of the work of Titus Livius, commonly referred to as Livy. While less than a third of the 142 books of his mighty *Ab Urbe Condita* remains, the magnitude of his work—which aimed, as that title would imply, to tell of all of the history of Rome from its foundation to the time of Augustus—means that a huge amount of what is known about the Romans comes mostly, and in many cases solely, from Livy. It is probably no exaggeration to suggest that Livy is a pillar by which the entire edifice of Roman historical scholarship is supported. Yet if the *importance* of Livy's work is essentially not questioned, its *excellence* occasionally is. As all who have made more than a passing investigation of his work will admit, Livy is an indispensable but far from perfect historian, and indeed the appraisals of his qualities in modern scholarship certainly do not hide (and may indeed dwell on) the deficiencies that are perceived to exist in his work. One of the areas in which he is often found to be wanting is in his discussion of military matters, which is of particular importance considering just how prominent war and warfare is in the *Ab Urbe Condita*. As Livy himself states, one of the main elements of his work is his chronicle of *per quos viros quibusque artibus domi militiaeque et partum et auctum imperium sit.*[1] The surviving portions of Livy indicate that this is no idle comment; indeed, as one scholar puts it, "Livy records and narrates more battles than any other ancient writer and for many of these his is the only surviving account."[2] Thus, real or suspected flaws in his presentation of *res militares* are of some significance towards Livy's reputation as a historian and can—and indeed ought to—limit just how reliable his history actually is.

Given these facts, it is perhaps not untoward to briefly describe some of these failings. One magisterial author dismisses Livy "as a narrator of battle" with the brutally simple statement that he is "beyond reclaim."[3] A later major analysis of Livy's work is of a similar opinion but is slightly more expansive about Livy's faults.[4] There is, first and foremost, a pervasive and, indeed, undisguised pro-Roman bias. Far from simple favoritism, it is claimed, Livy's need to glorify Rome caused him to distort, omit, or even alter facts about engagements in which Romans were worsted, with some massive defeats becoming Wellington's "near-run things." Moreover, in those defeats which Livy does allow himself to present as such, mishaps which may have occurred because of ill-considered battlefield decisions made by commanders whom the author himself wishes to praise were sanitized to remove the general's mistakes from the account.[5] Other detractions include Livy's abiding concern with style and readability, which weakens his discussion of war and battle when it leads him to elide important tactical details in some of his battle accounts for the sake of dramatic tension or clarity of expression.[6] In this manner, Livy's quest for elegance deprives his readers of facts necessary for a complete understanding of the operations. And if it is claimed that Livy was not doctoring his battle narratives or polishing them to the point of erasing crucial details, then he still managed to make significant blunders from sheer incompetence. Livy has a poor grasp of geography, which certainly diminishes his combat reports.[7] Moreover, he "certainly had no military experience; he is so ignorant of the practical aspects of soldiering that he can never have thrown a *pilum* in anger," and is claimed to have been so foolish as to claim that this weapon—the Roman heavy javelin—could be thrust as well as thrown.[8] In the pages of Livy, then, armies perform feats which no collection of soldiers of the time could reasonably have performed, their commanders conduct maneuvers which make no logical sense, and his battle-pieces read as if composed by a man who frankly had no idea how war was actually fought, presumably because he had never seen it for himself. Even scholars who are more generous in their criticism of Livy nevertheless attribute these kinds difficulties to him—according to the translator of the first Loeb volume of his text, Livy was "(n)either well informed nor specially interested in … the art of war."[9] Another critic, perhaps the most delicate of all (and, coincidentally, the only one who produced significant works of military history of his own), gently observes that "(t)he battle pieces of that admirable man of letters do not reveal just what we want to know."[10]

Such, at least, has certainly been the prevailing opinion of Livy as a military historian for the last seven decades at least. However, in recent years, this assessment has been subject to some scrutiny. First and foremost, many of the authors of these opinions have themselves softened the harshness of their judgment in the very works in which they offer it, usually on the grounds that Livy was apparently not writing for generals but for a far more general audience.[11] Secondly, the premise that Livy is a poor military historian almost always derives from passages in his text that contradict other written sources covering the same material. When this does occur, Livy is generally assumed to be less reliable than the other sources. However, an irresistible justification as to *why* these other sources are to be preferred is rarely furnished. Irritatingly circular logic then ensues. It is well-known that Livy is unreliable because he does not always compare well to other sources, which are more

reliable than Livy is. After all, it is well-known that Livy is unreliable; *quod erat demonstrandum*. Many of those who decry Livy's reliability note his Livy's treatment of the Second Punic War, which is contrasted to that of Polybius. Because the authority of Polybius is to be preferred (Livy, in fact, drew upon Polybius himself), such comparisons are almost always unfavorable. However, it is not infrequently the case that the only source to which Polybius *himself* can be compared is Livy. This process is then extended to other periods which Livy covers, even if the parallel source to which he is matched is not regarded as highly as Polybius is. Even if it may be conceded that Livy warps or mishandles the occasional notice from the Hannibalic War, and that Polybius is in every case to be preferred, Livy's text is of such enormity that a few bungled passages amidst his vast corpus might not necessarily reflect the whole text.

Lastly, Livy is often found wanting in his discussion of war and warfare because he has his soldiers perform exploits or describe the use of weaponry, which do not adhere to accepted wisdom about the capabilities of Rome's armies or the function of its arms.[12] Yet in no case is Livy cited with having men do things that would have been flatly *impossible*; in the pages of Livy, there is never a case when a Roman cavalryman lifts a battleship, for example, nor does any infantryman ever eat the sun. His men may occasionally do things that seem to defy conventional logic about how Roman soldiers are supposed to behave. Still, any historian with even a passing interest in war and

Statue of Roman historian Titus Livius at the Austrian Parliament Building. Titus Livius, known as Livy, was born in 59 BC and died in AD 17. He was a Roman historian best known for his monumental work Ab Urbe Condita, which chronicled the history of Rome from its legendary founding. [Photo by Bwag, CC BY-SA 4.0, via Wikimedia Commons]

combat can readily call to mind several episodes in the works of unimpeachably "reliable" historians in which the actions of men or use material departs from what is typically expected. Even the alleged howler about the incorrect use of the Roman javelin, offered as a succinct illustration of Livy's naïveté, inexperience, or ineptitude, has not incontrovertibly persuaded all modern historians of these defects. For one thing, Plutarch specifically mentions that *pila* were used in battle as thrusting weapons, a maneuver ordered by no less illustrious a commander than Julius Caesar himself.[13] Additionally, as another commentator on Livy points out, the bungle about the *pilum* seems to come from 9.19.7-8, where the operative phrase in Latin is *pilum, haud paulo quam hasta vehementius ictu missuque telum*. Because *ictus* is paired with *missus*, that sentence is often translated as "the javelin, a weapon more powerful thrust or thrown than a spear." It can, however, just as easily mean "the *pilum*, which is more powerful than a spear *on being thrown and finding its target*." The fact that Rome's heavy javelins could regularly pin two thick Greek *hoplon* shields together shows that this estimation is not a bad one for the relative levels of penetration a *pilum* could achieve when used for its main purpose, *id est* when it was thrown, which is precisely how Livy indicates they were deployed in the passage.[14]

Questions about Livy's competence (or, more specifically, the generally accepted lack thereof) have recently come under further investigation. However, there is certainly room for further inquiry of this sort. This may, perhaps, be explored more fully elsewhere. However, there remains that line of argument hinted at above; namely, that Livy's depiction of war is less than ideal, not because of what he *does* describe, but because of what he *does not*, and therefore "(t)he battle pieces of that admirable man of letters do not reveal just what we want to know." To put it another way—students of military history would find Livy frustrating (the argument runs), not because of the answers he provides, but because of the questions he elects—or neglects—to ask. It should be noted that this mild critique is the only one made by an actual modern student of ancient military history, as opposed to other scholars whose concerns are more philological in nature. It is also perhaps the one whose amplification is the most valuable—whether Livy's information is accurate is of no use if the information provided is not the right kind. Unfortunately, the author who respectfully offers it does not himself elaborate on how Livy may not be furnishing the right type of information. Nor, in fact, is such an analysis found in any of the other critics just mentioned, and even though, again, attempts are beginning to be made to "rehabilitate" Livy as a military historian, those attempts invariably focus on Livy's answers, not his questions. It may, perhaps, not be untoward to propose that such a study might be undertaken with profit.

Modern portrayal of Roman legionaries carrying pila. The pilum (plural: pila) was a heavy javelin used by Roman soldiers. It was about 2 meters (6.5 feet) long, with a wooden shaft and an iron shank ending in a pyramidal tip. Designed to penetrate armor and shields, it was thrown before close combat. Upon impact, the iron shank often bent, making shields unusable and preventing enemies from throwing the pila back. Roman legionaries carried two pila, launching them in volleys to disrupt enemy formations before engaging with their gladius. This tactic weakened opponents, leaving them vulnerable. The pilum was a key weapon in Rome's military dominance, evolving over centuries before being phased out in the 3rd century AD. [Wikimedia Commons]

II. Livy the Military Historian: What Kinds of Questions Does He Ask?

Thoughts of this kind, at least, have led to the beginnings of precisely such an investigation, the very early stages of which will be offered here. Yet a few things should be indicated before this appraisal begins. Firstly, this essay will avoid offering extensive commentary on the "truth" of what Livy narrates, especially through a synoptic comparison of that author with other ancients who relate some or all of the same events that he does. Again, such a task is itself not without merit, and a few works have begun to take steps in that direction. Still, such will not be attempted here—Livy's qualities as a military historian will be evaluated strictly based on what he says (or does not say) himself and will not be filtered through the prism of other sources. Secondly, a thorough investigation of all of Livy's books would easily overwhelm the space allotted to this piece and could easily fill volumes. For the present, therefore, books one through five—the so-called first "Pentad," encompassing the military history of Rome from the arrival of Aeneas to the departure of the Gauls after the sack of Rome in the fourth century—will be the object of survey.[15]

To commence—Livy, by his own account, was determined to write a history of the Romans and the deeds in peace and war that built their empire. The pages of books 1-5 of the *Ab Urbe Condita* are therefore filled with war and battles, describing 229 separate military engagements (defined for these purposes as an indication of violence in which a body of organized men who either were the authorized representatives of their communities, or who claimed to be such, fight another group of armed men representing another community). If, in Livy's descriptions of these 229 engagements and the wars of which they are part, there is not "just what we want to know"—if, another words, Livy does not ask the right questions—then an analysis of his treatment of this war-like ought to begin with precisely what questions he does ask to see how far short of what it is "we want to know" his lines of investigation are.

Drawing of the Macedonian Phalanx. The Macedonian Phalanx was a military formation developed by Philip II of Macedon and later employed by Alexander the Great. It consisted of heavily armed infantrymen known as phalangites, who wielded sarissas—long pikes measuring 15 to 21 feet (4.5 to 6.5 meters). The phalanx operated in tight, rectangular formations, with multiple rows of soldiers advancing in unison. This formation's advantages included its superior reach and strong frontal defense. Such a complex battlefield maneuver required highly trained phalangites. However, the rigid formation made it difficult to adapt to uneven terrain and left it vulnerable to cavalry or light infantry attacks on its flanks. Ultimately, Roman legions outmaneuvered the phalanx with their more adaptable formations. [Wikimedia Commons]

a) The Basics

Of all the things military historians might want to find in the reports of Livy, a few fundamental types of fact readily suggest themselves. It seems logical to assert that, at minimum, a modern scholar looking at the battles of Livy would reasonably expect to know who fought, when, where, and what the outcome of the combat was.

To all of these basic questions, Livy may generally be relied upon to give some answer; clearly, these questions concerned him, too. Proceeding to them severally—to the question of "who fought," Livy returns the names of the parties involved in all 229 cases, whether these parties be Roman or whether—as is the case in seventeen of these clashes—Livy is discussing wars waged between other people which would have affected the Romans (such as, for example, the battles between the Etruscans and the Gauls in Book 5).[16] To the question of *when* these parties fought, Livy's answers are slightly more nuanced. This is because, despite the title given to his work (which may not have been the one its author had bestowed upon it), Livy very rarely uses "ab urbe condita" (or "years from the foundation of the city") to date events in Books 1-5. The first of these books, after all, recounts the wars fought in Italy's mythic past throughout the end of the Roman monarchy, including four fought centuries before the city was founded in 753 BCE.[17] For the battles fought during the monarchy, far more common are indications in the text of times *terminus ante quem*, such as the

nine led by Romulus Rex, which must have been fought between the foundation of the city and the forty years given as the length of his reign 1.15.7).[18]

Beginning in Book 2 (which coincides with the foundation of the Republic), Livy typically provides the names of the chief magistrates in office at the time when an event occurred to provide chronological context. Since in Livy's time these could be compared to the *Fasi Capitolini* (lists of these magistrates known to have been but in public places), for the 190 battles outlined in Books 2-5, Livy furnishes reasonably precise dates for all but fourteen of them.[19] Of the remaining fourteen, two were mentioned earlier—namely, they are the battles between the Gauls and Etruscans in Book 5, ones that seem to have occurred at a time which Livy himself apparently did not know precisely.[20] The others are found between Chapters 39 and 40 of Book 2, discussing the vengeful rampage of the exiled Coriolanus against the city, which happened at some time after 491, the year of his banishment, and 487.

Next: to the matter of *where* these battles were fought, Livy, again, almost always has an answer—for 197 of the 229 battles in Books 1-5, Livy provides some indication of the where it transpired, either by identifying a specific place or by giving enough in the full narrative description of hostilities for a reasonable guess for the location to be made. Finally (and perhaps most importantly), for only three battles across the expanse of Books 1 through 5 does Livy not mention an outcome, so few that each can be briefly mentioned.

The first of these is conveyed in 2.8.6, where Livy mentions that the consul fought the city of Veii, but does not explicitly mention or even allude to what happened. More complicated is the battle in 4.26.6, which at first glance is fairly straightforward—Livy mentions that "some sources" pass along that the Aequi and Volsci were met on the Algidus river, and that their defeat of the Romans by the consuls led to the appointment of a dictator. However, the previous several sentences cast doubt on whether a battle actually occurred, and whether the unusual amount of time taken by the generals to entrench and train led to the recall of the consuls. Finally, in 4.30.14, Livy notes that there was a battle against the Veientines and Fidenates at Nomentum, and while it was followed by a truce, it is left ambiguous whether the Romans won, lost, or were held to a draw. For the other 226 engagements, Livy supplies either an implicit or explicit statement as to what had happened, even if merely noting that the battle had been inconclusive.

b) Specifics

In general, then, Livy fairly consistently provides his readers with the bare minimum of who fought, when, where, and to what outcome, in the battles he mentions. Beyond these fundamentals, however, his details are less abundant. For example, while Livy often furnishes particulars as to why the combatants in the battles he describes took to arms, he omits such reasoning for almost a quarter of them (57 out of 229 battles). If he gives any *casus belli* at all for these 57, it comes in the form of a desultory "ru-mors reached Rome that some enemy was preparing for war, and the Romans marched against them." Once war is declared, Livy offers practically nothing about what the specific strategic role, if any, these battles play in the wars of which they are constituents, generally contenting himself with conflating the cause of the war with the objectives of fighting. To put it another way, if (for example) the Romans went to war because their territory has been ravaged by the Aequi, Volsci, or Sabines (against some combination of whom the Romans fought practically all of the battles discussed in Book 3), then the strategic objectives of the battles that resulted were to repel and avenge the invasion. In only six instances throughout Livy's five books there are variations from this formula. Four of these six involve wars declared without provocation in Book 1, of which one was a battle fought by king Tullus Hostilius for apparently the sole purpose of fighting a successful war (1.22.1-1.25.14), and three were fought by Ancus Marcius, apparently to capture prisoners to increase Rome's population (1.33.4-5). The other two are in Book 2, where the Latins, bound by treaty obligations to the Romans, sought permission to fight the Aequi who had invaded their lands. The Romans instead fought the Aequi for the Latins, for the sole purpose—Livy claims—of keeping the Latins from becoming too comfortable with fighting their own enemies and reaffirming their dependence on Rome (2.30.7-9; 2.31.4-6).

In a similar vein, when actual combat is joined, Livy is decidedly selective about the details of operations he tends to include. For instance, if the battle he is documenting is one fought by Romans, Livy will almost always identify the commander of the Roman side. For only thirty-six of these engagements does Livy fail to do so, and almost every one of these battles either involved a raid on Roman territory (in which the Romans are not combatants, but victims of aggression), or occurred during the period when the Romans experimented with a magistracy called "military tribunes with consular power." Since anywhere from three to eight of these could be elected in a year, Livy will sometimes fail to specify which one was in command during the particular battle. By contrast, he is far less apt to include the name of an enemy captain, such that of all the battles fought by the Romans in Books 1-5, only fourteen enemy commanders are named.[21] Indeed, of these fourteen, no fewer than five were themselves at one point Roman: Titus Tatius, L. Tarquinius Superbus, Arruns Tarquinius, Titus Tarquinius, and Gnaeus Marcius Coriolanus.

About the soldiers themselves, Livy has even less to say (or so it appears at first glance). If it is a commonplace that ancient authors grotesquely exaggerate the numbers of participants in the battles they record, Livy might well be the exception, at least in Books 1-5. This can be asserted because there is frankly nothing to exaggerate: in only nine battles in Books 1-5 does Livy offer any indication of the numbers of participants involved at all. Of these nine, for three of them only the number of Romans are given (2.30.7-9, 2.31.1-3, 2.50.1-11), and in five others, it is the

merely numbers of the enemy that are included (3.18.4-9, 4.57.7, 4.59.3-10, 5.32.3, 5.32.4).[22] In only one confrontation are numbers passed along for both sides (2.30.10-15, when the Romans are described as having fielded three legions' worth of men against the Volsci, and their enemy is held to have marshalled the exact number). And if Livy is reticent about the number who take part, he is equally reticent about those who fall. In just eight episodes, Livy conveys the approximate number of casualties. For three of these, it is only the Roman slain who are numbered: the two Horatii brothers, who died facing the Curiatii triplets in the regal period (1.22.1-1.25.14); the 305 members of the *gens Fabia* who die in their private war with Veii in 477 (2.50.1-11); and the 5,800 Romans who died across several battles with the Hernici in 464 (3.4.7-8, 3.5.5-9, 3.5.10-11). The enemy dead are only given in four engagements outside of the aforementioned Curiatii triplets who fell against the Horatii (the dead of the Aequi and Volsci who fell in the two encounters discussed in 3.5.1-3; 13,470 more Volsci killed in 3.8.6-11; and 7,000 more Aequi killed in 3.31.3-4).

If Livy rarely numbers the soldiers in his reports, he somewhat more frequently takes note of what "branch of the service"—if the term may be forgiven—they fought; thirty-six of his battle reports mention that cavalry was involved to varying extents.[23] On the other hand, he is particularly reticent—almost maddeningly so—about whatever weapons and armaments they may have used. Although *use* of weapons is portrayed quite frequently in Livy, the weapons themselves are almost never named; instead, Livy uses generic terms like *tela* (for weapons of all kinds) and *ferrum* (literally "iron," the Roman equivalent of "cold steel"), and has his soldiers protected by *arma* (literally "arms" in a non-anatomical sense). Only fourteen times does Livy directly name any of these *tela* or *arma*, in which instances naming the *gladius* or sword four times, the *hasta* or thrusting spear five times, and *parma* or cavalryman's shield twice.[24] The remaining four notices involve words which usually mean "javelins," namely *pilum* (2.30.10-15; 2.45.1-2.47.9; 2.65.1-6) and *verutum* (2.20.9). Yet only once, when a *verutum* is being employed, are these weapons being treated as missile weapons; each mention of the *pilum* sees it used, not as a javelin, but as a spear. There are several possible explanations for this. One is that the *pila* were indeed being used as thrusting spears, a function that they could perform (see above). Another may be that Livy used a term for "javelin"—*pilum*—to mean "spear," in much the same way as modern audiences might mention "throwing" spears (even though "spear" properly refers to a stabbing weapon which stays in the hand), and that this was a stylistic choice rather than one dictated by ignorance about which was which. As far as weapons borne by the army as a whole, Livy describes the use of siege engines—and names those engines—a total of three times: once in the context of the siege of Pometia in 502 (2.17.1-7), once in discussing a siege of Fidenae in 435 (4.22.2-6), and once in his description of the lengthy campaign to besiege Veii

from 405-396 (5.1.1-7.13).

Once the battle finally commences, Livy typically provides a straightforward account of what transpires. Certain incidentals are typically omitted, however. Livy almost never mentions the time of year in which a battle occurs, for example, and does so only twice (both in discussion of battles waged in Rome's mythic past by its founder-king Romulus: 1.5.7-1.6.2; 1.9.10 - 1.10.2). Nor does he often mention the time of day, either; in only seventeen reports is the specific time of day given for a single engagement.[25] Livy is generally loath to note the duration of a particular battle, doing so only 41 times and almost always to note when an engagement lasted for more than one day. Finally, in only 27 battles does Livy mention any geographical feature of the field on which the battle occurs, and in every case, the feature is mentioned because it plays a direct role in the battle.

III. Conclusions

The foregoing sought to reexamine Livy, often regarded as a poor military historian, and determine if, at the very least, he endeavors to pose the right kind of questions, regardless of how sound the answers he provides are. It is far from a complete survey: after all, questions of the type outlined above are not the only ones which might be sought in Livy's text, and there are many others which Livy ought to ask for "(t)he battle pieces of that admirable man of letters" to "reveal just what we want to know." Furthermore, the First Pentad (under survey here) represents just a little over a thirtieth of what Livy had once written and is not quite a sixth of what remains. Additionally, the period encompassed by that First Pentad was a time when the Romans did not write history as it is now known, largely contenting themselves with producing yearly notices of a few sentences in length which briefly summarized the events of the year (the first acknowledged Roman historian, Fabius Pictor, would not start writing more expansively on Rome's past until the 200s BCE).[26] Hence, even if Livy had wanted to be more fulsome in his account of Rome's wars, it can be doubted whether he would have found much more information to include. Finally, more research (currently in progress) will be needed to determine whether the treatment of war and warfare in the First Pentad represents its treatment by Livy in the whole (or at least the remaining parts) of the *Ab Urbe Condita*. Nevertheless, it is reasonable to venture that, if the First Pentad is indeed a representative enough sample, Livy as a narrator of battle is hardly beyond reclaim, and that in fact he goes far toward being able to tell the modern historian much of what he, she, or they might want to know.

About the Author

Seth Kendall is an Associate Professor of History at Georgia Gwinnett College. His interest is Republican Roman History, a field in which his previously published work is situated. He is currently working on an extensive analysis of Livy and warfare.

References

Adcock, Frank. *The Roman Art of War Under the Republic*. New York: Barnes & Noble Inc., 1960.

Burck, E. "The Third Decade." In *Livy*, edited by T.A. Dorey(editor), 21-47. London: Routledge and Kegan Paul, 1971.

Foster, B.O. "Introduction." In *Livy in Fourteen Volumes I: Books I and II* (B.O. Foster, trans.), ix-xxvi. Cambridge, MA: Harvard University Press, 1919.

Frier, Bruce W. *Libri Annales Pontificum Maximorum: The Origins of the Annalistic Tradition*. Ann Arbor: University of Michigan Press, 1999.

Koon, Samuel. *Infantry Combat in Livy's Battle Narratives*. Oxford: BAR Publishing, 2016.

Luce, Torrey. *Livy: The Composition of His History*. Princeton: Princeton University

Press, 1977.

Syme, Sir Ronald. *Tacitus*. Oxford: Clarendon Press, 1958.

Walsh, Pastrick. *Livy: His Historical Aims and Methods*. Cambridge: Cambridge University Press, 1961.

Endnotes

1   Preface of Book 1, section 9. For context, the slightly expanded reference is: *Ad illa mihi pro se quisque acriter intendat animum ... per quos viros quibusque artibus domi militiaeque et partum et auctum imperium sit* ("To these matters may the reader pay particular attention ... through what men and by what methods in peace **and in war** [emphasis added] was Rome's power born and increased").

2   Samuel Koon, *Infantry Combat in Livy's Battle Narratives* (Oxford, UK: BAR Publishing, 2016), 23.

3   Sir Ronald Syme, *Tacitus* (Oxford, UK: Clarendon Press, 1958), 156.

4   Much of what will be discussed in the paragraph to follow is the opinion of Patrick Walsh, *Livy: His Historical Aims and Methods* (Cambridge: Cambridge University Press, 1961), with specific citations below.

5   For a discussion of such "patriotic distortions" see Walsh, *Livy*, 98-99, 105.

6   Walsh, *Livy*, 197-201, 204.

7   Walsh, *Livy*, 153-157.

8   Walsh, *Livy*, p. 4 (for the conclusion that Livy never experienced combat, though this is an inference rather than a conclusion based on any literary source that explicitly confirms this lack of experience), 157-158 (mentioning the *pilum* specifically), and 143 (though Walsh suggests that is the result of a mistranslation from the Greek of Livy's sources).

9   B. O. Foster, "Introduction." In *Livy in Fourteen Volumes I: Books I and II* (B.O. Foster, trans.), ix-xxvi. (Cambridge, Massachusetts: Harvard University Press, 1919), p. xxvi. Burck agrees (E. Burck, "The Third Decade." In *Livy*, edited by T.A. Dorey(editor), [London: Routledge and Kegan Paul, 1971], p. 38), noting that "expert knowledge and little interest in detailed accuracy by Livy has long been proven in the spheres of military life, strategic planning, battle reports and the nature of siege operations," as does Luce (Torrey Luce, *Livy: The Composition of His History* [Princeton: Princeton University Press, 1977], p. 41), who declares that "Military maneuvers per se did not particularly interest him."

10 Frank Adcock, *The Roman Art of War Under the Republic* (New York: Barnes & Noble Inc., 1960), pp. 8-9.

11 So Burck, *loc. cit.;* Walsh, *Livy*, 159. Similar is Luce, *Livy*, xvii.

12 Walsh (*Livy*, 143) notes two fairly egregious examples. The first (which Walsh does not cite but is from Livy 38.7.10) involves the Romans besieging Ambracia, who had resorted to dig a mine under its walls and attempted to use a barricade against counterminers made out of doors. This appears to be Livy attempting to make sense of Polybius 22.28, where the miners and counterminers protected themselves with large square sheilds (θυρεός in Greek. This word descends from the Greek θύρα (door), so it is easy to see how that might have been mistranslated. However, it is *also* possible that Livy's version is the correct one, since the same Polybius passage also mentions that combatants protected themselves with "wicker-work" (γέρρον), which, which can mean "oxhide shields" but far more commonly means "wattled screens from the marketplace." Romans and Ambraciots could easily have used improvised materials to block each other, just as Livy says. The second "howler" (for which Walsh again does not give citation) is a comparison of the final stage of the battle of Cynoscephalae, found in Livy 33.6.1-33.10.10 and Polybius 18.20-27. At the climax of this battle, Macedonian King Philip orders his reinforcements to do *something* with their spears and charge downhill against the Romans and rescue the men already engaged. Polybius uses a verb form of καταβάλλω, which can mean "lower" (in the sense of level) but can also mean "throw down; discard." This latter is how Livy recounts it (*hastis positis*), which is said to be an error of translation and inexperience; after all, why would a phalanx ever discard their spears, the primary weapon of that formation? Except even the text of Polybius provides a possible answer: the Macedonian *sarissa* was over fifteen feet in length, and with these cumbersome weapons soldiers were being asked to charge downhill (into their own troops, whom they were to rescue) after a thunderstorm the night before, which would have rendered the ground slippery and treacherous (as Polybius himself explicitly states). An attack with swords – far lighter and more maneuverable) might in fact make perfect sense here. Nor does the misunderstood gesture of surrender Polybius reports – that the Macedonians raised their spears, their king having retired – invalidate this hypothesis, as Polybius directly states that this action was performed by Macedonians who had reached the summit in their flight (and who could thus have easily resumed their spears, perhaps precisely so they could make this sign of surrender). Livy himself seems to suggest that these unfortunates were a reserve who had never been sent down the hill at all, thus without *hastis positis*. Thus, in both of these cases Livy may not have "mistranslated" Polybius nor had the "temerity" to correct him (Walsh's word; Luce, *Livy* 39 also states that this is happening with Livy's depiction of Cynoscephalae) but was presenting a version which diverges from Polybius but is not nonsensical for that.

13 Plutarch, *Pompeius* 69.2-3; *Caesar*, 45.

14 Koon, *Infantry Combat,* 24 (which also references one of the passages of Plutarch mentioned above). However, see below about Livy's use of *pilum.*

15 Livy's use of five-book Pentads to organize his work is explored extensively by Luce, *Livy*, beginning with page xviii. Walsh, *Livy*, 5-8 also provides lengthy discussion of these, as do several of the contributors to Dorey, *Livy*.

16 Battles such as those found in 1.1.3; 1.1.5-9; 1.2.1-3; 1.2.5; 1.5.3-4; 1.5.7-1.6.2; 1.7.1-3; 2.14.5; 2.14.6-9; 2.53.1-3; 2.53.4-5; 3.7.5; 4.10.5; 5.34.9; 5.35.2; 5.36.5-8; and 5.45.1-3.

17 Found in 1.1.3, 1.1.5-9, 1.2.1-3, 1.2.5. Three others include two fought by supporters of Romulus and Remus against Alba Longa (1.5.3-4, 1.5.7-1.6.2), as well as another between the followers of Romulus and those of Remus, with its tragic result (1.7.1-3).

18 However, it seems that this was an approximation, as the reign of Romulus is states as having been thirty-seven years in 1.21.5. Similar dating ranges are used for all the subsequent later kings; for example, the three wars fought by Tullus Hostilius must have happened during his reign, given as having begun eighty years after the first year of Romulus (as Romulus is claimed to have ruled for thirty-seven years, as was noted above, and his successor Numa Pompilius to have done for forty-three as mentioned in the same spot) and lasting for thirty two years (1.22.8).

19 Modern readers can be guided by these magistrates, as well, since the existing fragments of the *Fasti* have allowed for their reconstruction to reasonable completeness.

20 5.34.9; 5.35.2.

21 Amulius, Titus Tatius, Mettius Fufetius, Arruns Tarquinius, Lars Porsenna, Octavius Mamilius, L. Tarquinius Superbus, Titus Tarquinius, Gnaeus Marcius Coriolanus, Attius Tullius, Cloelius Gracchus, Aequian named Cluilius, Lars Tolumnius, Brennus.

22 In fact, of these the total number of the enemy is directly stated only once (3.18.4-9); the others mention merely the number of prisoners taken, from which the enemy strength can (somewhat imprecisely) be extrapolated.

23 1.12.1-1.13.1; 14.4-11; 1.27.4-11; 1.30.4-10; 1.37.1-4; 1.37.5-6; 2.6.4-2.7.3; 2.17.1-3; 2.19.3-20.13; 2.25.1-2; 2.25.3-4; 2.25.5; 2.26.1-3; 2.31.1-3; 2.42.3-4; 2.43.7-10; 2.45.1-2.47.9; 2.49.9-12; 2.53.1-3; 2.53.4-5; 2.65.1-6; 3.22.3-9; 3.23.3-6; 3.28.1-10; 3.69.8-3.70.14; 4.17.10-19.8; 4.26.11-29.5; 4.32.8 - 34.7; 4.37.6-39.9; 4.47.1-4; 4.47.5; 5.1.1-7.13; 5.28.8-13; 5.32.3; 5.32.4; 5.39.1-42.18.

24 Swords: 1.22.1-1.25.14; 2.30.10-15; 2.45.1-2.47.9; 4.37.6-39.9; spears: 1.27.4-11; 2.6.4-2.7.3; 2.19.3-20.13; 2.45.1-2.47.9; 4.17.10-19.8; cavalryman's shield: 2.45.1-2.47.9; 4.37.6-39.9.

25 1.11.5-9; 1.12.1-1.13.1; 2.26.1-3; 2.51.6; 2.59.6-11; 2.64.8-11; 3.28.1-10; 3.60.1-61.10; 3.61.10-63.4; 4.9.14-10.4; 4.37.6-39.9; 5.26.3-8; 5.28.8-13; 5.45.1-3; 5.45.4-8; 5.45.8; 5.47.1-7.

26 This is the theme of Bruce Frier's *Libri Annales Pontificum Maximorum: The Origins of the Annalistic Tradition*. (Ann Arbor: University of Michigan Press, 1999).

The Red Stick War 1813–1814

Dr. Matt Meador

University of Tennessee Martin

ABSTRACT

The Red Stick War (1813–1814), often overshadowed by the broader War of 1812, represented both a Creek civil war and a decisive moment in U.S. expansion into the Southeast. Sparked by divisions within the Creek Confederacy between accommodationist Lower Creeks and traditionalist Upper Creeks, also known as Red Sticks, the conflict embodied the struggle between cultural preservation and assimilation under mounting U.S. pressure. Inspired by Tecumseh's call for pan-Indian resistance and fueled by spiritual revival, the Red Sticks launched attacks that culminated in the Fort Mims massacre, prompting a full-scale U.S. military response under General Andrew Jackson. Key battles at Tallushatchee, Talladega, Emuckfau Creek, and ultimately Horseshoe Bend shattered Creek resistance, leading to the Treaty of Fort Jackson and the cession of over 21 million acres of land. The war accelerated the decline of Creek sovereignty, deepened internal divisions, and set a precedent for future U.S. policies of removal and displacement. This study situates the Red Stick War within the dual context of Native resistance and American expansionism, arguing that it was not merely a regional conflict but a transformative episode that reshaped the political and cultural landscape of the 19th-century American South.

Keywords: Red Stick War, Creek Confederacy, Creek Civil War, Andrew Jackson, Horseshoe Bend, Treaty of Fort Jackson, Tecumseh, Native American resistance, U.S. expansionism, Southeastern frontier, War of 1812, Creek sovereignty, U.S. Removal policy, Fort Mims Massacre

La Guerra de los Bastones Rojos, 1813-1814

RESUMEN

La Guerra de los Bastones Rojos (1813-1814), a menudo eclipsada por la Guerra de 1812, representó tanto una guerra civil creek como un momento decisivo en la expansión estadounidense hacia

doi: 10.18278/mhc.2.2.3

el sureste. Desatado por las divisiones dentro de la Confederación Creek entre los Creek Inferiores, acomodaticios, y los Creek Superiores, tradicionalistas, también conocidos como Palos Rojos, el conflicto representó la lucha entre la preservación cultural y la asimilación bajo la creciente presión estadounidense. Inspirados por el llamado de Tecumseh a la resistencia panindia e impulsados por un renacimiento espiritual, los Palos Rojos lanzaron ataques que culminaron en la masacre de Fort Mims, lo que provocó una respuesta militar estadounidense a gran escala bajo el mando del general Andrew Jackson. Las batallas clave en Tallushatchee, Talladega, Emuckfau Creek y, finalmente, Horseshoe Bend, desmantelaron la resistencia creek, lo que condujo al Tratado de Fort Jackson y a la cesión de más de 21 millones de acres de tierra. La guerra aceleró el declive de la soberanía creek, profundizó las divisiones internas y sentó un precedente para las futuras políticas estadounidenses de expulsión y desplazamiento. Este estudio sitúa la Guerra del Palo Rojo en el doble contexto de la resistencia indígena y el expansionismo estadounidense, argumentando que no fue simplemente un conflicto regional, sino un episodio transformador que transformó el panorama político y cultural del sur de Estados Unidos del siglo XIX.

Palabras clave: La Guerra de los Bastones Rojos, Confederación Creek, Guerra Civil Creek, Andrew Jackson, Horseshoe Bend, Tratado de Fort Jackson, Tecumseh, resistencia indígena, expansionismo estadounidense, frontera sureste, Guerra de 1812, soberanía creek, política de expulsión de EE. UU., Masacre de Fort Mims

1813年至1814年的红棍战争

摘要

1813年至1814年发生的红棍战争常常被更广泛的1812年战争所掩盖，它既是一场克里克族内战，也是美国向东南疆域扩张的决定性时刻。这场冲突源于克里克邦联内部主张迁就的下克里克族与主张传统的上克里克族（也称为红棍族）之间的分裂，体现了在日益增长的美国压力下，克里克族在文化保护与同化之间的斗争。在特库姆塞号召全印第安人抵抗的鼓舞下，在精神复兴的推动下，红棍族发动了进攻，最终导致了米姆斯堡大屠杀，这促使安德鲁·杰克逊将军率领的美国军队进行全面反击。在塔卢沙奇、塔拉迪加、埃木克福克里克以及最终的马蹄湾战役中，克里克族的抵抗被粉碎，最终促成了《杰克逊堡条约》的签订，克里克族割让了超过2100万英亩的土地。这场战争加速了克里克族主权的衰落，加深了内部分裂，并为美国未来的驱逐和流离失所政策开创了先例。本研究将红棍战争置于原住民抵抗和美国扩张主义的双重情境中，认为它不仅仅是一场地区冲突，更是重塑19世纪美国南部政治和文化格局的变革性事件。

关键词：红棍战争，克里克邦联，克里克内战，安德鲁·杰克逊，马蹄湾，《杰克逊堡条约》，特库姆塞，美洲原住民抵抗，美国扩张主义，东南边疆，1812年战争，克里克族主权，美国驱逐政策，米姆斯堡大屠杀

Introduction

The War of 1812 is generally studied in the broader context as a conflict between the United States and Great Britain over territorial control of the Northwest Territory and maritime rights. However, in 1813–1814, another conflict in the southeastern U.S. involving the powerful Creek Confederacy fighting its own Civil War would fall to an opportunistic American force led by General Andrew Jackson during tensions with international powers along the coastal region. Many factors fueled the engine of this conflict, ultimately leading to open hostility between the Creek Confederacy and American troops. The early 19th century experienced a new resistance from Native Americans towards American expansion. Efforts by Shawnee leader Tecumseh and his brother Tenskwatawa, "The Prophet," led to a significant initiative to unify native tribes into a confederation for a common cause. For Tecumseh, a world in which white men expanded meant the death sentence for each native tribe, individually, one after another, unless a unified front was presented to stop expansion. Tecumseh's dream was the "uniting of campfires." Therefore, along with his brother, he began speaking to neighboring tribes to return to the old ways in the Native lands of the Northwest and Southeast around 1810.[1] There was no communication over long distances except for traveling to each tribe along the path and gaining buy-in one by one to this common cause. After visiting the neighboring Chickasaw and Choctaw and failing to gain support, Tecumseh found a spark in the attitudes of some Creek Confederacy leaders to take up a more traditional way of life.[2]

During the post-Revolutionary War period, the Creek Confederacy faced increased pressure from American expansion as the population of new settlers grew in Georgia, but this pressure multiplied as new lands were acquired west of Creek territory in places like the Mississippi Territory, which included present-day Mississippi and the port area of Mobile along the Tensaw and Tombigbee Rivers. Additionally, the admission of the States of Louisiana (1812) and Tennessee (1796) into the Union secured the expansion of American settlement and commerce in those states. U.S. interaction and engagement with the Creek leadership was conducted by Colonel Benjamin Hawkins, the United States Representative to the Creeks; Hawkins devised a "plan of civilization," destabilizing traditional tribal customs in four areas. First, Hawkins's plan transformed the roles of men and women. Second, the Confederacy was to adopt American norms, abolish communal field usage, and, finally, accept private land holdings for commercialization.[3] By 1811, the powerful Creek Confederacy population was divided on the issue of American expansion, thus splitting into two factions. The Lower Creeks, in towns such as Coweta, Cusseta, Eufaula, Hitchiti, Okmulgee, Okfuskee, Ochessee, and Apalachicola, advocated for accommodating Americanization (Headmen from these towns became members of the Creek National Council). The traditional faction, the Upper Creeks, also known as Red Sticks, took on Tecumseh's vision, and this faction was determined to resist American expansion.[4] A civil war resulted amongst the Confederacy from 1813 to 1814, thus allowing American forces to engage the tribe while the opportunity was there. Furthermore, the war marked a turning point in Native American resistance in the Southeast, thus accelerating the loss of Creek sovereignty and paving the way for future U.S. policy of removal and displacement. This article explores the origins of the Red Stick War, high-lights key themes, events, and battles, and explores the lasting consequences of the Red Stick War, shedding light on how this conflict influenced the broader struggle for Native American autonomy and reshaped the American South in the 19th century.[5]

The Creek Confederacy

Creeks weren't a tribe, *per se*, but a confederacy of tribes with a long lineage in the Southeastern region of North America. Creeks were a matrilineal society, yet multi-ethnic and multi-lingual, consisting of Muskogee, Hitchiti, Alabama, Yuchi, Natchez, Tuckabatchie, and Shawnee, among others. Creeks were centrally located in present-day Alabama and Georgia. However, the Confederacy controlled most of Florida at its height of power, along with access to land and trade networks as far west as the Mississippi River, North to the Great Lakes and Ohio Valley, and east into the Appalachians and the southeastern Atlantic coastline. The Creek Confederacy was vast; an estimated 25,000 people lived in the territory by the 1800s.[6]

The Creeks are topically categorized into two geographical divisions based on early European encounters: the Upper and Lower Creeks. Despite the complexity of social and political dynamics that formed over time among the Creek Confederacy, geography makes the divisions easy to understand.[7] Upper Creek towns in the Muskogee region were 200 miles inland, along the Coosa and Tallapoosa Rivers. Their extensive tributary network was crucial for the British, who referred to them as "Creeks."[8] Upper Creek towns resisted outside encroachment into Creek land and culture, seeking to preserve traditional ways of life, as the Prophet and Tecumseh encouraged. Thus, Upper Creeks were hostile to American expansion, and anyone friendly or supportive of Americans. Alternatively, the Lower Creeks were much closer to American settlements in Georgia, along coastal areas of Spanish Florida, cities such as Mobile, and up the Tensaw and Tombigbee Rivers. The Lower Creek region increased the adoption of European American customs through trade and settlement interactions, leading to the early support of initiatives offered by foreigners (see Map 1).[9]

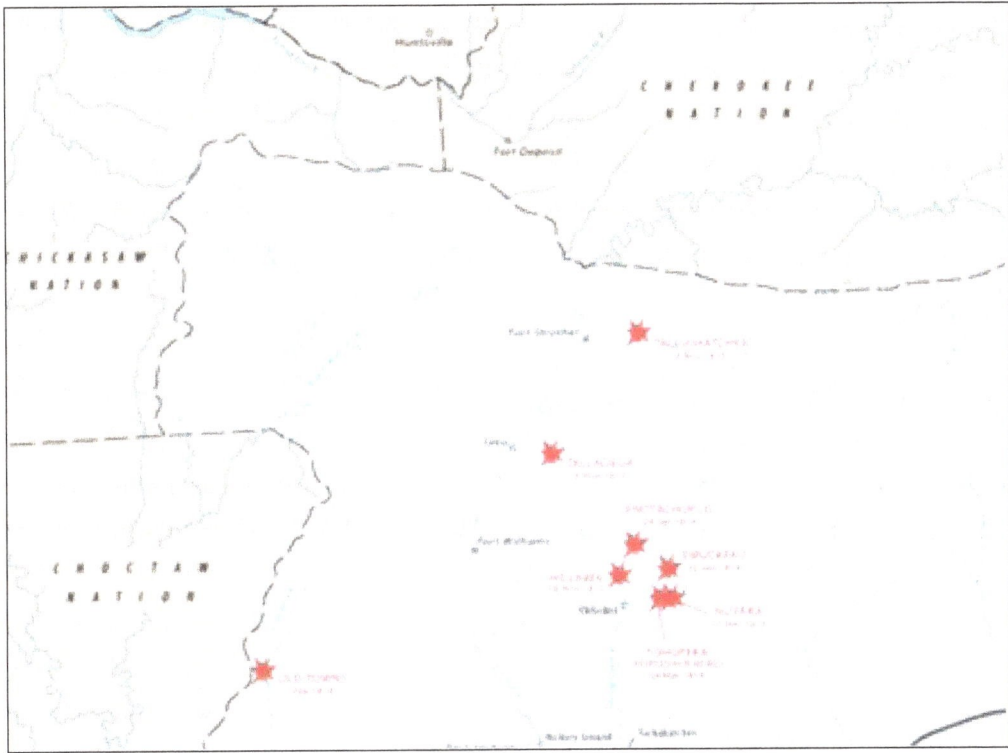

Map 1. "Map of Battle Sites in the Creek War (1813–1814)," adapted from Richard D. Blackmon, *The Creek War, 1813–1814* (Washington, D.C.: U.S. Army Center of Military History, 2004).

The Creeks' matrilineal clan system shaped social, political, and cultural life. Clan inheritance was passed through the mother's line, and every Creek individual belonged to their mother's clan for life. These clans, such as the Wind, Bear, Deer, Tiger, Beaver, Panther, Snake, and others, governed identity, marriage, and social responsibilities. Clan membership determined rules for behavior, particularly concerning marriage (as marrying within one's clan was forbidden), and influenced an individual's role in the Creek society.

Clans played a vital role in governance, spiritual practices, and justice, with clan representatives contributing to town councils and setting a standard for determining peace or war.[10] Each clan was considered a family responsible for protecting and supporting its members. In times of conflict, clans helped organize warriors and oversaw justice for offenses committed against or by their members. This system fostered strong communal bonds and ensured the survival of traditions and values.

"Towns" formed the nerve centers of the Creek Confederacy. Creek Towns were autonomous and governed by a "Mico," or chief, and a council of elders. Towns, or Talwa, were designated as red, or war, towns, and white, or peace, towns. Red and White towns also had additional "Headmen," which included the Tustunnuggee (War Chief) and Heniha (Speaker). Red and White towns were in both the upper and lower divisions of the Creek territory. A stick was also a Red or White town designation, and members of each town were called Red Sticks or White Sticks. Additionally, a town could transition from Red to White or White to Red based on the most males.[11] Male children were identified early in life as either extroverted or introverted. For example, extroverted males were encouraged to become warriors, and introverted males were encouraged to study medicine. When Red Sticks and White Sticks experienced leadership changes, white towns selected a Red Stick Mico for a Red Town, and Red Sticks selected a White Stick Mico for White Towns.[12]

Forging Relationships (1755–1813)

European encounters, relationships, and interactions in the Southeast are recorded in the 16th century. The Spanish expeditions through Florida and the heart of the Southeast to the Mississippi River led to French, British, and eventually American interaction with Natives in the Southeast. Over time, each international entity vied for influence over the Creeks and their neighboring tribes via trade, commerce, and war. Relationships were strengthened or weakened based on what impacted the Creek territory. One documented instance of this going back to the mid-18th Century was the Cherokee-Creek War. Red Sticks in Upper Towns were outraged that sick warriors returning from an expedition to Charlestown with British Agents, which resulted in the Treaty of Charlestown of 1749. French leaders urged the Creeks not to trust the British, who allied with the Cherokee. The Cherokee permitted the Senecas' passage through their lands into Creek lands, thus violating the treaty. For several years (1749–1755), the Creeks and Cherokee fought each other, destroying towns, killing hunters, or raiding each other in the Georgia backcountry. Hostilities halted due to European expansion into the region.

Throughout the 1760s and again in the 1780s, Creeks asserted power through international prowess with international forces, making their way to Havana, Cuba, via ferry on Cuban boats. The relationship bore fruit as

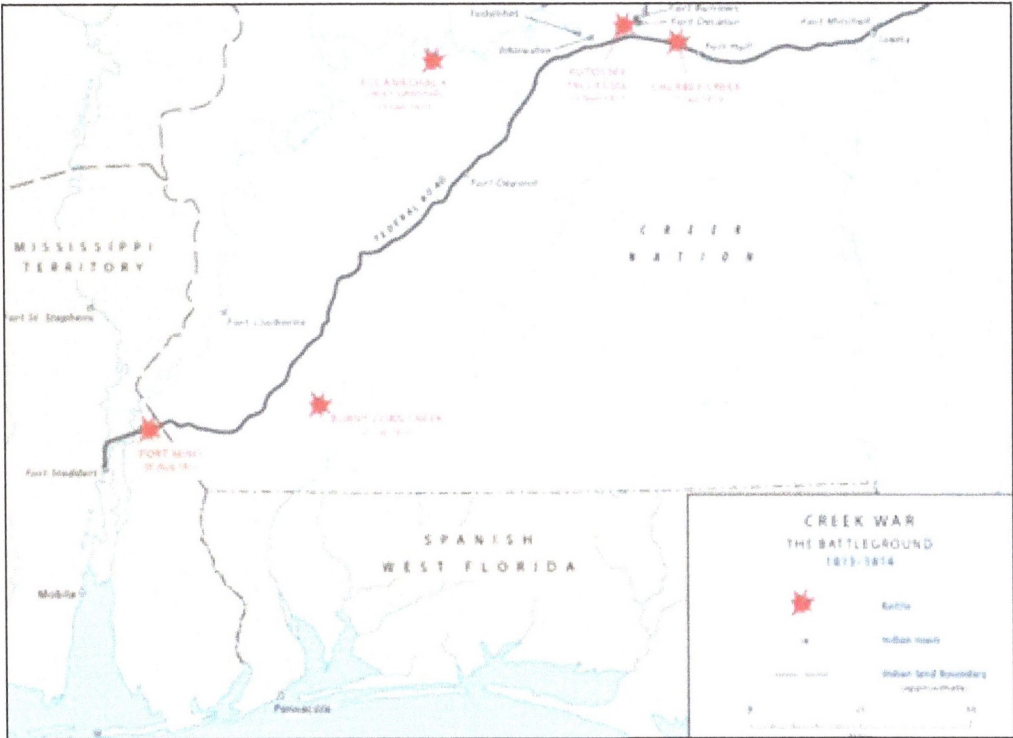

Map 2. "Map of Battle Sites in the Creek War (1813–1814)," adapted from Richard D. Blackmon, *The Creek War, 1813–1814* (Washington, D.C.: U.S. Army Center of Military History, 2004).

Map 3. "Creek Nation and Federal Road, 1813," adapted from Richard D. Blackmon, *The Creek War, 1813–1814* (Washington, D.C.: U.S. Army Center of Military History, 2004).

Creeks and Spanish Cubans frequented coastal destinations for trade freely.[13] However, after geopolitical realignment from the Seven Years' War in 1763, Creeks feared British aggression against them, versus the Spanish and French, and localized its advantages through diplomatic means, with the British having started by sending an envoy to Charles Town, South Carolina, to have conversations.[14] British trade was demanding and unscrupulous. In 1765, the Creeks and Choctaws went to war, and the British Agent, John Stuart, sent weapons and ammo to the Choctaw to occupy the Creek and prevent Red Stick assaults against British settlement in the Georgia backcountry until the American Revolution began. Creek families no longer received gifts nor had access to Spain and France, leaving them indebted to traders' demands.[15] Geopolitics was predominant between Britain and Spain, and the Creek supported it throughout the American Revolutionary period. During the 1780s Franco-Spanish dispute, Spain encouraged the idea of arming and supplying the Creek Indians to aid in destabilizing British operations.

Creek authority over its lands was respected by those governments they encountered. The Creeks maintained a rich history as farmers and hunters, primarily of deer, which resulted in overhunting to trade with European powers. The deer pelt trade was highly demanding, and Creeks expanded their economic empire into new areas in Florida in search of skins. Thus, Creeks dominated most, if not all, political interaction among European coun-

tries by lending them land within their territory and routinely enforcing the understanding that it was not European land.[16] In Pensacola, Creeks asserted that Spanish authority was not recognized over Creeks; when the British took over Spanish posts in Pensacola and St. Augustine, Creek and Seminole leaders highly encouraged the British to remain along the coast and not venture out into the land.[17] Taking this approach ensured Creek autonomy, and the lands remained a conditional borderland.

External Pressures and Internal Divisions

Evidence of external pressure and internal divisions among the Creek Confederacy is seen from the onset of the Franco-Spanish conflict. Lower Creeks supported the Spanish in retaking posts occupied by the British, and the Upper Creek, Choctaws, and Seminoles (related to the Creek) assisted in defending British positions.[18] European settlements of Britain and Spain along the Gulf Coast continued to widen this internal void as the encounters with the Lower Creeks continuously happened, unlike with the Upper Creeks. Treaties between the Creeks and Britain or between the Creeks and Spain set boundaries around trade and commerce, military assistance, land rights, and mutual defense. Leverage Creeks, built with European governments, now included another entity to cooperate with, and a worldview of autonomy evolved into a new, more significant identity crisis as Creeks shifted to policy agreements focused on survival. Before the American Revolution, Lower Creek Mikos ceded land near Lower Creek towns in the Georgia colony. However, Upper Creek leadership openly disputed any agreement because of their lack of involvement in the disposition, thus leading to attacks on settlements in the Georgia backcountry.

Alexander McGillivray, a half-blooded Creek, acquired considerable wealth through plantation ownership after the American Revolution in 1783. Georgia's backcountry exploded with new settlements, and the American population now impacted Lower Creek. McGillivray used influence and power to unite the Creek towns over the new American government, signing the Treaty of New York in 1790, first for the Cusetahs and 23 other Creek town leaders.[19] The 1790 treaty recognized Creeks as the "Masters of their own country," having title to their lands and respect from the U.S. Government. The agreement between the Creeks and the U.S. Government outlined peace and friendship to Upper and Lower Creeks, acknowledged U.S. protection, established boundaries along the Oconee River in Georgia for U.S. settlement, and set annual payments to the Creeks for trade goods and services. Additionally, the Treaty of New York (1790) outlined the behaviors of each party in the event of injustices or violence. It included that Creeks advise U.S. agents of any intentions of themselves or neighboring tribes designed to target the U.S. or its interests.

U.S. Agent Colonel Benjamin Hawkins, appointed by President Wash-ington in 1796, initiated programs and endeavors aimed at Creek assimilation under the "civilization plan." Lower Creeks were receptive to American initiatives; several Creek leaders and families made fortunes owning plantations for farming. The National Council of Creeks was formed to comprise Upper and Lower Creek towns, and the council was responsible for managing treaties and diplomacy for the Creek Confederacy. Additionally, diplomatic negotiations in 1796 resulted in the signing of the Treaty of the Creeks, also known as Colerain, thus defining boundary lines and establishing trading or military posts in regions designated by the U.S.

The early 19th century presented unprecedented American expansion fueled by economic interests in commercializing land for profit. The Creek National Council faced additional external pressure in subsequent treaties, such as the Treaty of Fort Wilkinson (1802) and the Treaty of Washington (1805). The Treaty of Washington, signed on November 14, 1805, resulted in a massive land cession in present-day Georgia (see Map 1). The newly ceded lands included a swath of territory between the Oconee and Ocmulgee Rivers, excluding a small tract roughly 3 miles by 5 miles where the Ocmulgee Old Town was located; the region was rich for farming and coveted by American settlers. The Treaty of Washington also established the federal road, a significant source of contention and a divisive topic between the Upper and Lower Creeks. In exchange, the United States promised to pay the Creeks $200,000 in annuities and provide supplies, such as livestock and tools, to support their transition program to an agrarian economy promoted by Benjamin Hawkins.[20]

Another treaty indirectly impacting the Creek Confederacy was the Treaty of Fort Wayne, signed on September 30, 1811. The Fort Wayne Treaty included land cessions in the Old Northwest (present-day Indiana, Illinois, and Michigan). It characterized a broader pattern of U.S. treaty-making, involving similar themes of Native American land and internal tribal divisions. Territorial Governor William Henry Harrison negotiated the treaty, which involved land cessions totaling more than 3 million acres, and several tribes, including the Delaware, Shawnee, and Miami, signed the treaty. The Treaty of Fort Wayne inspired Tecumseh and his brother, who argued that no single tribe had the authority to cede land. Tecumseh traveled extensively to speak and unite tribes against the United States and to resist further land cessions. Tecumseh's effort culminated in building up Prophetstown in the Northwest Territory, the center of Native resistance, ranging in size from 650 to 3,000 warriors, some of whom were Creek tribe members.[21] This was not the first instance of Shawnee's outrage at American authority; in 1793, there was anger and violence over acculturation. However, he urged supporters to resist American expansion and unite to defend their lands, significantly impacting the Red Sticks' attitudes toward Americans and tribal supporters.[22]

Upper Creek leadership was found through Red Eagle or William Weatherford. Tecumseh worked with Red Eagle, mentored him, and saw his leadership capability.[23] Weatherford was half-blooded (Creek mother and Scottish father) but lived the life of the Creeks. Red Eagle's hometown, Coosada, is in Lower Creek territory. His mother was a Princess from the Wind Clan; therefore, he was royalty by default. There was no higher clan than the Wing Clan, and he maintained the highest influence on the Creek Confederacy, but he was also an advocate of raising the Red Stick.[24] Red Eagle's involvement with the Red Sticks was rooted deep in tradition. Through Red Eagle's insistence, The Shawnee Prophet "inspired" several Creek Prophets who then spiritually fueled young warriors of Upper Creek Towns. Josiah Francis, or Hillis Hadjo, was chosen and spent almost two weeks in isolation before the Creek Prophet proclaimed visions and supernatural abilities. The Creek Prophet supported spiritual warfare and resistance to assimilation.

A fully inspired Upper Creeks' spiritual awakening and spiritual revival was underway, and Josiah Francis called for the purification of Creeks, acknowledging that a Great Spirit would protect them from Americans and anyone embracing assimilation. Upper Creek Prophets viewed this as a fight to preserve their traditions, land, and sovereignty, which made this impending crisis a holy war, and they shared this sentiment with their peers.[25] While a spiritual awakening occurred in Upper Creek towns, Tecumseh continued to travel regionally among Creek towns and attempted to inspire as many Creek leaders as possible to raise the Red Stick with Red Eagle. Headman Tustinnuggee Thlucco, or Big Warrior, received and welcomed Tecumseh, but he could not inspire him to raise the Red Stick. Circumstances were not that Big Warrior supported Americans, but he foresaw the destruction of the Creek Nation because of a war. For Red Sticks, the goal was simple: destroy the National Council and remove foreign, illegitimate, American legal and political sentiment that built the council's foundation.[26]

By 1812, the U.S. was at war with Britain. British forces, preoccupied with France, recognized that the Indians were valuable enough to cause problems for Americans, so they promised aid in return for open rebellion.[27] A conflict between Americans and the British was a sign that Upper Creeks would benefit from an alliance with the British in the long run. This was, in fact, a fear for the U.S. Government. President Madison was more concerned about Spanish than British activities in the southern United States. For the U.S. Government, the fear was a European power riling up Southern Indians and the British being allowed to use West Florida and the ports of Mobile and Pensacola to stage and launch attacks on New Orleans.[28] Madison preliminarily asked for U.S. troops to mobilize against West Florida. Major General Jackson raised 2,000 Tennessee militia to reinforce New Orleans. Additionally, the U.S. Government expanded the Federal Road through Creek land to increase military supply traffic from the east into the Mississippi Territory.

After the Battle of Tippecanoe, Creeks engaged in open hostilities on roads leading into Creek territory; Americans were singled out as the target of violence since the roads that Creeks attacked were occupied by the increased presence of settlers entering Creek territory on these roads. Pressure mounted externally and internally for the Creek Confederacy over acts of violence committed by Creeks or U.S. citizens and how justice would be served. Per the Treaty of New York, the Creek National Council was responsible for the justice of crimes committed by Creeks within the sovereign territory. A new paradigm was the legitimacy of the Creek National Council to bring justice to those who committed crimes outside Creek boundaries. This was tested as an envoy of Upper Creeks, returning from visiting the Shawnee in the North, who assaulted and killed settler families in Tennessee; these crimes were quite heinous and led to the immediate demand to have those responsible brought to justice by American standards. Colonel Hawkins reminded the National Council of the treaty of 1796 and demanded swift action for further acts of violence, meaning that those responsible be brought to justice. Hawkins informed that Upper Creeks would not be brought alive and insisted that the legal principle was to bring criminals to justice. Thus in January of 1813, Jackson began moving troops in two forces. First, Jackson's main force moved via the Cumberland, Ohio, and Mississippi Rivers, where this force met with the second column of cavalry under Colonel Coffee, who traveled via the Natchez Trace. Both forces were in or near the capital of the Mississippi Territory when Jackson received word that the strategy had changed, and West Florida was no longer within the scope of U.S. interest.[29] Jackson began demobilizing his force and began the march back to Tennessee from the Mississippi Territory in March 1813.

Concurrently, acts of violence from the Upper Creeks were designated a "war on American settlers" in general terms by Upper Creek headmen. Around March 1813, the Tuskegee Warrior and Little Warrior of Upper Creek towns advocated violence on settlers; in this instance, a pregnant woman was murdered, her child removed from her womb, and her womb impaled on a stake. Hawkins decried, "Of any act of savagery towards the U.S., this is most outrageous."[30] Hawkins proclaimed these incidents were not random, asserting that headmen encouraging violence speak for the entire Creek Nation. The National Council sought to maintain the friendship established with Americans. Still, Upper Creeks did not wish to maintain a National Council, even plotting to kill anyone friendly or supportive of Americans. In June 1813, Red Sticks had amassed support for raising the Red Stick against those who did not support them. Red Sticks gathered their forces at the fork of the Coosa and Tallapoosa Rivers, where they executed several Creeks who adhered to Hawkins's policy on justice. There, the Red Sticks decided to destroy the national Creek capital, Tuckabatchee, and the Lower Creek capital, Coweta.[31]

Raising the Red Stick (1813–1814)

By the summer of 1813, the Creek Confederacy was in a Civil War. Red Sticks began planning and preparing full assaults on Creek towns that opposed them, along with American settlements. Rumors circulated widely in the region about the Red Sticks and their supply network, including British and Spanish sources. President Madison ordered General Wilkinson at New Orleans to capture Mobile to prevent the British supply of the Creeks. Mobile was captured without any incident and, in doing so, left Pensacola as the principal supplier of weapons and ammunition to Creek forces.[32]

Upper Creeks, led by a Creek prophet, Latecau, went to Coosa and invited any leader from the National Council who had hesitations to support the Red Sticks to come and participate in conversations. Through dances and spiritual movements, Latecau attempted to convert the hesitations into support from these headmen. Instead, there was an attack, and three headmen were killed. In retaliation, headmen who escaped gathered their warriors and attacked on Coosa. During the engagement, Latecau himself was killed along with eight of his companions, and then the National Council Creeks moved on Ofuskee to target more Red Sticks.[33]

The first engagement between Red Sticks and American forces occurred at Burnt Corn Creek (see Map 2). A group of Red Sticks, led by Peter McQueen, traveled to Pensacola, Flor-

Image 1. "Massacre at Fort Mims," engraved by Alonzo Chappel, 1857. In *History of the Indian Tribes of North America*, Library of Congress, Washington, D.C.

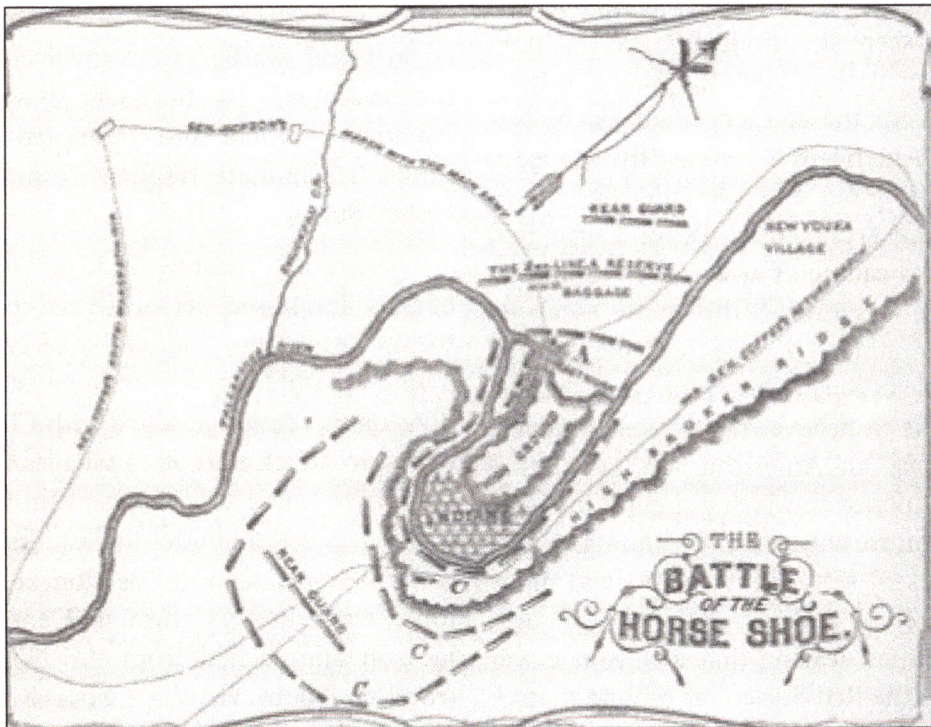

Map 4. "Map of the Battle of Horseshoe Bend," in Richard D. Blackmon, *The Creek War, 1813–1814* (Washington, D.C.: U.S. Army Center of Military History, 2004).

ida, to secure arms and ammunition from the Spanish Governor. On the way back to Upper Towns, a U.S. militia force under Colonel James Caller ambushed the Red Sticks near Burnt Corn Creek. Initially, the U.S. forces successfully controlled the engagement, but the Red Sticks regrouped and counterattacked, forcing the militia to retreat in disorganized fashion. The battle heightened the senses of many people living in that region. American officers felt that the Red Sticks were attempting to "broaden" the war and use these supplies and ammunition against settlers.[34]

Ammunition and arms the Red Sticks received came from the Spanish, who were coerced into believing that the Red Sticks would aid the Spanish if an American invasion occurred; since they had just surrendered Mobile, the deal seemed appealing.[35] The U.S. government played into the fears of settlers by using the savagery of attacks by Native Americans to leverage the chance of carrying out much broader operations in the area.[36] After Burnt Corn, Red Stick headmen saw that the U.S. militia force was a direct threat and escalated their attacks against settlements. The Battle of Burnt Corn motivated the Red Sticks to believe they were formidable against an American foe, concreting confidence and laying the groundwork for future engagement planning. A U.S. loss sent settlers into panic, and many packed up and moved to fortified communities, fearing that a full-scale war with the Red Sticks was among them.[37] The Battle of Burnt Corn was a Red Stick victory, and Red Eagle immediately planned a strike against Ft. Mims

in the Tensaw District.

The most infamous event of the Red Stick War occurred at Fort Mims. Fort Mims consisted of a makeshift stockade near the confluence of the Alabama and Tombigbee Rivers. (see Map 2) Rising tensions forced settlers and Lower Creek allies to flee there, fearing attack. Several hundred families of Lower Creeks and settlers, along with their slaves, made their way to Fort Mims for protection. On August 30, 1813, around 1,000 Red Stick warriors under Peter McQueen, Red Eagle, Josiah Francis, and other headmen attacked Fort Mims. In two waves of attack, Red Sticks set fire to Fort Mims and killed hundreds of settlers and mixed-blood Creeks; no quarter was given to those who could not escape, and women and children who were not usually targeted in Creek warfare were involved in the slaughter.[38] The massacre shocked American settlers and prompted an immediate military response from the United States.

General Andrew Jackson, now back in Tennessee, personally accepted the opportunity to lead a force of 2,500 Tennessee militiamen from the western division of Tennessee, allied with Cherokees, to attack Red Stick villages.[39] A section of the East Tennessee militia was also called up under the leadership of Gen. Cocke, and this section of the force made its way through Georgia. Jackson approached from the North, traveling South via the Coosa River. The force established Fort Strother inside Creek territory as a supply position for further engagements with Red

Sticks. Meanwhile, Jackson sent General John Coffee with about 900 troops to attack Tallushatchee.[40] American forces encircled the city and launched an all-out assault, killing approximately 200 Red Stick warriors. Women and children were also among the casualties, and the town was destroyed. Creeks, not Red Sticks, were impressed with the American force and offered support via loyalty to the U.S. Tallushatchee demonstrated Jackson's brutal counter-insurgency, thus intensifying the war, and displayed the implementation of allied Native American forces, such as the Cherokees, and loyal Creeks who opposed the Red Sticks.[41]

Shortly after Tallushatchee, Jackson received word that a group of pro-American Creeks (Lower Creeks) were besieged by 1,000 Red Sticks at Fort Leslie at Talladega. Red Eagle proclaimed that all inside would perish if they did not join the Red Sticks in warring with U.S. forces.[42] Jackson marched 2,000 Tennessee militia and engaged the Red Sticks in battle. While *en route* to Talladega, General Cocke recalled his force back to Western Georgia. However, this was not communicated until after the recall started, and Ft. Strother was left with limited protection. The Red Sticks found a weakness in the U.S. force at Talladega, taking advantage of it to escape annihilation.[43] After fierce fighting, the U.S. and Creek allies defeated the Red Sticks, killing approximately 300 warriors. The victory relieved Creek supporters of American forces and further weakened the Red Stick faction.[44] The battle was another significant victory for Jackson, reinforcing

his military reputation and demonstrating the effectiveness of combined American and Native forces against the Red Sticks. The tactics of American officers were based on lessons learned from previous victories. For example, American troops formed a semicircle around the Red Sticks at Tallahatchie and Talladega, lured them to attack, and then surrounded them. The Creeks of the Hillabee towns pledged their allegiance to U.S. forces, and Jackson promised that there would be no military action against them. However, that promise was void as the East Tennessee Militia attacked those Creek towns in the North. The Creeks there were defenseless. Jackson suggested Cocke was utterly insubordinate. The Hillabee Creeks declared war on U.S. forces as a result.[45]

The Georgia and Mississippi Militias were involved in the offensive on the Red Sticks through a U.S. response. When General Floyd's Georgia men were supplied and ready to march, they moved into Fort Lawrence along the Federal Road in the Lower Creek region the same day General Coffee defeated Red Sticks at Tallushatchee. From Ft. Lawrence, Floyd's 1,500 troops and cannon battery marched on Coweta, surrounded by Red Sticks, in November of 1813. Red Sticks gave up their siege when they learned of the U.S. force bearing down on Coweta.[46] Floyd's army crossed the Chattahoochee River and established Fort Mitchell, which acted in the same capacity as Fort Strother, established by Jackson. The towns of Autosee and Tallasee were targets for the Georgia Militia column.

During the assaults, they killed the chiefs. General Floyd employed the strategy of surrounding the towns, but this strategy was not acted out. After the artillery barrage, a bayonet assault cleared the towns; Creeks were also allowed to ransack the villages before burning them.[47] Floyd, after recuperating from a wound to his knee, marched his troops back, and the Red Sticks harassed them. Red Sticks used communication to determine the movement of the militia and vacated the towns before militia surrounded the town. Such was the case for Nuyaka; when Georgia militia entered the town, it was empty. Thus, the town was burned, and the militia traveled back to Georgia.[48]

A third column of militia comprised the Mississippi Militia, which operated from the Mississippi Territory. General Claiborne was ordered to lead about 700 militia and Choctaw warriors, led by Pushamataha, up the Alabama River. Fort Claiborne was established up the Alabama River between Mobile and present-day Montgomery.[49] From Fort Claiborne, Choctaw Chief Pushamataha and several warriors assaulted Red Sticks at Burnt Corn Creek, disrupting communication with Pensacola. In November 1813, a target was selected for engagement: The Red Stick Holy Ground, Eccanachaca. Like other militia terms, the Mississippi Militia enlistments were running out, and Winter was coming. The offensive on Eccanachaca involved an 80-mile march and rugged terrain to navigate upon the arrival of U.S. forces, which

Image 2. "William Weatherford's Surrender to Andrew Jackson," in Richard D. Blackmon, *The Creek War, 1813–1814* (Washington, D.C.: U.S. Army Center of Military History, 2004).

now included U.S. Regulars and militia. Claiborne's force engaged the town in a three-sided attack on Eccanachaca and overwhelmed Red Sticks, with 33 killed, who escaped across Alabama or fled elsewhere. U.S. forces searched for people, while the Choctaw were permitted to burn the town. The force was also allowed to burn or destroy anything that could aid the Red Sticks in continuing the conflict.[50] Claiborne raided one of Weatherford's (Red Eagles) plantations before returning to Fort Claiborne. The U.S. regulars were all left with active orders to fight Red Sticks, so the force and Chickasaw warriors attacked Red Stick towns North of Fort Claiborne, up to Tuscaloosa, but the towns were empty.

In January 1814, governmental support for the conflict and the enlistments of militiamen were growing short; therefore, Jackson marched his command into the heart of Upper Creek territory and fought at Emuckfaw Creek and Enotachopco Creek, claiming several hundred more Creek casualties at those battles. At Emuckfaw Creek, Jackson's forces were attacked by a large Red Stick War party. Though the Americans repelled the assault, Jackson's force incurred heavy casualties. Two days later, at Enotachopo Creek, Jackson's army was ambushed again while attempting to retreat. Again, suffering heavy losses, Jackson managed to withdraw successfully and regroup. These battles demonstrated that the Red Sticks remained a formidable force and that defeating them would require more excellent military resources.

The Red Stick War's strategically decisive battle occurred at Horseshoe Bend on the Tallapoosa River, where the Red Sticks fortified a defensive position. Jackson led 3,300 men, including Tennessee militia, U.S. Regulars, Cherokee warriors, and Lower Creeks into their positions. The Red sticks, numbering around 1,000, were trapped in a river bend, with their only escape route blocked. After bombarding the Red Stick fortifications, Jackson's troops stormed the position. Cherokee and Lower Creek allies attacked from the rear, cutting off Red Stick escape routes.[51] The battle resulted in a massacre of Red Stick warriors, with over 800 killed and only a few escaping. Horseshoe Bend effectively ended the Red Stick War. The massive defeat shattered the resistance, and its leaders, including William Weatherford, surrendered to American forces.

Following the Red Stick defeat, a negotiated peace occurred in the U.S. Government on August 8th, 1814. The Treaty of Fort Jackson, overseen by Andrew Jackson, required the Creeks to cede 21 million acres of land to the United States. The treaty was meant to punish the Red Sticks. Still, the conditions of land cessation also impacted the pro-American Creeks who had fought alongside the U.S. Members of the National Council were present for negotiations. There was no involvement in the settlement; Jackson dictated the settlement. The treaty marked the beginning of large-scale U.S. expansion into the Deep South, laying the groundwork for the forced removal of Native Americans in the 1830s.

Map 5. "Creek Nation and Territory Ceded by the Treaty of Fort Jackson, 1814," in Richard D. Blackmon, *The Creek War, 1813–1814* (Washington, D.C.: U.S. Army Center of Military History, 2004).

Legacy of the Red Stick War

The Red Stick War left a profound legacy on Native American sovereignty, U.S. expansion, and the political landscape of the Southeast. An internal Creek civil war, influenced by growing tensions over American encroachment and cultural divisions, had far-reaching consequences that shaped the future of the Creek people and the American South. One of the most immediate legacies of the Red Stick War was the devastation of the Creek Nation. The war resulted in the deaths of thousands of Creek warriors and civilians, the destruction of villages, and the disintegration of the future of the Confederacy. Perhaps most consequential was the Treaty of Fort Jackson (1814), where the Creek Nation ceded over 23 million acres of land to the United States. This cession, which included lands belonging to both hostile and allied Creeks, severely diminished Creek sovereignty and opened vast territories for American settlement in present-day Alabama and Georgia.[52]

The war also exacerbated internal divisions within Creek society. The conflict between the "Red Sticks" (traditionalists who opposed American influence) and the more progressive faction (aligned with the National Council and American interests) left a lingering fracture. The defeat of the Red Sticks and the suppression of traditionalist beliefs marked a shift toward greater assimilation, as surviving Creeks faced mounting pressure to adopt American customs and agricultural practices.[53] For the United States, the war had significant implications for westward expansion. The victory not only secured valuable land but also signaled a broader policy of aggressive expansionism

and dispossession of Native lands. The war helped elevate Andrew Jackson's national reputation, setting the stage for his later political career and controversial Indian removal policies in the 1830s.[54]

Conclusion

The Red Stick War contributed to the erosion of Native American political autonomy. The weakening of the Creek Nation symbolized the broader decline of Native power in the Southeast. It also foreshadowed future conflicts and forced removals, including the infamous Trail of Tears in the 1830s, which culminated in the relocation of thousands of Native Americans west of the Mississippi River. In conclusion, the Red Stick War's legacy was marked by loss and transformation—the loss of land, sovereignty, and cultural independence for the Creek Nation and the acceleration of American territorial expansion. It is a critical chapter in the broader narrative of Native American resistance and the inexorable advance of American imperialism.

About the Author

Matt Meador, Ed.D., is a Program Manager for FedEx in Memphis, TN. For the last fifteen years, Matt's central focus has been customer-driven design, development, implementation, and evaluation of training (project/program management) and performance platforms. As an adjunct history professor, Matt remains active in the educational and history community by teaching virtual and hybrid history courses for Southwest Tennessee Community College and UT Martin. Matt is currently writing several articles for the 2023-2024 calendar year intended for publication on higher education curriculum and instruction performance assessment, dimensional assessment and data interpretation, learning analytics as connecting the characteristics of a learning organization, and segments of Memphis regional history. Matt's research interests include the Learning Organization Framework Model, performance evaluation, leadership development, innovation studies beyond blended learning, and the history of Memphis. Matt has an off-duty supervisor of 13 years and five children.

Bibliography

Black, Jason. "Memories of the Alabama Creek War, 1813–1814: U.S. Governmental and Native Identities at the Horseshoe Bend National Military Park." *American Indian Quarterly* 33, no. 2 (Spring 2009): 200-229.

Blackmon, Richard D. *The Creek War, 1813–1814*. Washington, D.C.: Center of Military History, United States Army, 2014.

Braund, Kathryn. *Tohopeka*. USA: University of Kansas, 2011.

Braund, Kathryn. *Deerskins and Duffels: The Creek Indian Trade with Anglo-America, 1685–1815*. Tuscaloosa: University of Alabama Press, 1993, 100–102, 104–118.

Bunn, Mike, and Clay Williams. *Battle for the Southern Frontier: The Creek War and the War 1812*. USA: History Press, 2008.

Carter, Clarence. "British Policy toward the American Indians in the South, 1763–8." *English Historical Review* 33, no. 129 (1918): 37–39, 44–49.

Coker, William S., and Thomas D. Watson. *Indian Traders of the Southeast Spanish Borderlands*. Pensacola: University of West Florida Press, 1986, 7–8.

Corkran, David H. *The Creek Frontier, 1540–1783*. Norman: University of Oklahoma Press, 1967, 58–59, 229–248, 253–254, 273–278.

Dowd, Gregory. *A Spirited Resistance: The North American Indian Struggle for Unity, 1745–1815*. Baltimore: Johns Hopkins University Press, 1992.

Edmunds, R. David. *Tecumseh and the Quest for Indian Leadership*. Boston: Pearson, 2008.

Eggleston, George. *Red Eagle: Wars with the Creek Indians of Alabama*. USA: Kessinger, 2006.

Fixico, Donald. "The Spiritual Balance of Peace in the Red Stick War, 1813–1814." In *People's Peace: Prospects for a Human Future*, edited by Yasmin Saikia and Chad Haines, 65–84. Syracuse: Syracuse University Press, 2019.

Halbert, H. S., and T. H. Ball. *The Creek War of 1813 and 1814*. Tuscaloosa: University of Alabama Press, 1969.

Hassig, Ross. "Internal Conflict in the Creek War of 1813–1814." *Ethnohistory* 12, no. 3 (Summer 1974): 251–271.

Han, H. Daniel. *The Invention of the Creek Nation, 1670–1763*. Lincoln: University of Nebraska Press, 2004, 115–119.

Hickey, Donald. *The War of 1812: A Forgotten Conflict*. Chicago: University of Illinois Press, 1989.

Hine, Robert, and John Mack Farragher. *The American West: A New Interpretive History*. New Haven: Yale University Press, 2000.

"Congress at Pensacola with the Upper and Lower Creeks," May 26–June 4, 1765. In *Early American Indian Documents: Treaties and Laws, 1607–1789*, Vol. 12, *Georgia and Florida Treaties, 1776–1776*, edited by John T. Juricek, 256–273. Frederick, MD: University Publications of America, 2002.

Kokomoor, Kevin. *Of One Mind and Of One Government: The Rise and Fall of the Creek Nation in the Early Republic*. Lincoln: University of Nebraska Press, 2018, chap. 10.

Marquis, Christopher. "Judge Andrew Jackson, Presiding." *American History* 41, no. 1 (April 2006): 40–46.

Nunez Jr., Theron. "Creek Nativism and the Creek War of 1813–1814." *Ethnohistory* 5, no. 2 (Spring 1958): 131.

O'Brien, Sean. *In Bitterness and Tears: Andrew Jackson's Destruction of the Creeks and Seminoles*. USA: Globe Pequot, 2005.

Owsley, Frank. *Struggle for the Gulf Borderlands: The Creek War and the Battle of New Orleans, 1812–1815*. USA: University of Alabama, 2000.

Remini, Robert V. *Andrew Jackson and His Indian Wars*. New York: Viking, 2001.

Richter, Daniel. *Facing East from Indian Country: A Native History of Early Amer-*

ica. Cambridge: Harvard University Press, 2001.

Saunt, Claudio. *A New Order of Things: Property, Power, and the Transformation of the Creek Indians, 1733–1816*. Cambridge: Cambridge University Press, 1999.

Silver, Timothy. *A New Face on the Countryside: Indians, Colonists, and Enslaved People in South Atlantic Forests, 1500–1800*. Cambridge: Cambridge University Press, 1990.

"Treaty of New York" concluded on August 7, 1790, between the United States and the Creek Nation. In *Indian Affairs: Laws and Treaties*, edited by Charles J. Kappler, vol. 2, 25–29. Washington, D.C.: Government Printing Office, 1904.

"Treaty of Colerain," concluded on June 29, 1796, between the United States and the Creek Nation. In *Indian Affairs: Laws and Treaties*, edited by Charles J. Kappler, vol. 2, 39–41. Washington, D.C.: Government Printing Office, 1904.

"Treaty of Fort Confederation," concluded on June 16, 1802, between the United States and the Creek Nation. In *Indian Affairs: Laws and Treaties*, edited by Charles J. Kappler, vol. 2, 65–67. Washington, D.C.: Government Printing Office, 1904.

"Treaty of Washington," concluded on November 14, 1805, between the United States and the Creek Nation. In *Indian Affairs: Laws and Treaties*, edited by Charles J. Kappler, vol. 2, 89–93. Washington, D.C.: Government Printing Office, 1904.

Waselkov, Gregory A. *A Conquering Spirit: Fort Mims and the Redstick War of 1813–1814*. Tuscaloosa: University of Alabama Press, 2006.

Waskelov, Gregory. *Conquering Spirit: Fort Mims and the Redstick War of 1813–1814*. Alabama: University of Alabama Press, 2009.

Wright, J. Leitch. *Creeks and Seminoles: The Destruction and Regeneration of the Muscogulge People*. Lincoln: University of Nebraska Press, 1986, 111–112.

Endnotes

1   Eggleston, George. Red Eagle and the Wars with the Creek Indians of Alabama.

2   Braund, *Tohopeka: Rethinking the Creek War & the War of 1812*, 1. Daniel Dupre suggests that Tecumseh, the Prophet, and the militant faction of Creeks were loosely aligned despite the distance between the two nations. See Dupre, The Creek War, 211. Some literature suggests that Creek warriors, albeit small, were in the Northwest, with Tecumseh having allied with travelers South.

3 Braund, 1.

4 Marianne Mills, foreword to Tohopeka, xiii, suggests that the Southeast region of the U.S. post-Revolution was defining its identity as diverse people joined to fight for a new country. She notes that the Creek Nation was the largest and most influential tribe in the Southeast from the late 18th century to the early 19th century.

5 The Redstick War (1813–1814) is often framed as a civil war within the Creek Nation, as the division between the traditionalist Redsticks and the more accommodationist Lower Creeks created internal strife. However, this interpretation overlooks the broader context of American expansionism and how U.S. policies exacerbated these divisions. The Redsticks' resistance was not merely a rejection of Lower Creek leadership but also a rejection of previous treaties that ceded Creek lands to the United States Government—often without the consent of much of the Creek population. For a deeper analysis of these internal divisions, see Claudio Saunt, *A New Order of Things: Property, Power, and the Transformation of the Creek Indians, 1733–1816* (Cambridge: Cambridge University Press, 1999), 185–189.

6 Fixico, 67.

7 Ibid, 40.

8 Fixico, Donald. Balance of Peace in the Red Stick War, pg. 67. Also see Eggleston, George. *Red Eagle and the Wars with the Creek Indians of Alabama,*1897.

9 Blackmon, Richard. The Creek War; 1813–1814, Center of Military History, U.S. Army, Washington, D.C., 2014, pg. 8.

10 Swanton, John R. (October–December 1912). "A Forward on the Social Organization of the Creek Indians." *American Anthropologist.* 14 (4): 593–599.

11 Ethridge, Robbie (2003). *Creek Country: The Creek Indians and Their World.* Chapel Hill, North Carolina: The University of North Carolina Press. pp. 95–96, 102.

12 Ethridge, pp. 95-96

13 Hill, 38.

14 Bartram (1848).

15 Braund, Kathryn, Deerskins and Duffels, 100–102, 104–18; Clarence Carter, "British Policy toward the American Indians in the South, 1763-8," *English Historical Review* 33, no. 129 (1918): 37–39, 44–49; William S. Coker and Thomas D. Watson, *Indian Traders of the Southeast Spanish Borderlands* (Pensacola: University of West Florida Press, 1986), 7–8; Corkran, Creek Frontier, 58–59, 229–48, 253–254, 273–78; Han, Invention of the Creek Nation, 115–19; J. Leitch Wright, *Creeks and Seminoles: The Destruction and Regeneration of the Muscogulge People* (Lincoln: University of Nebraska Press, 1986), 111–12.

16 Braund, Kathryn, Deerskins and Duffels, The Creek Indian Trade with Anglo-America, 1685–1815, (Lincoln University of Nebraska Press, 1996), 67–70.

17 "Congress at Pensacola with the Upper and Lower Creeks," May 26–June 4, 1765, in John T. Juricek, ed., Early American Indian Documents: Treaties and Laws, 1607–1789, vol 12., Georgia and Florida Treaties, 1776–1776 (Frederick, Md.: University Publications of America, 2002), 256–73.

18 Hill, 64.

19 Treaty of New York, (1790). *Indian Affairs* (Vol 11), pg. 25.

20 The Washington Treaty of 1805.

21 Source—Creek in Prophetstown.

22 Kevin Kokomoor, *Of One Mind and Of One Government: The Rise and Fall of the Creek Nation in the Early Republic* (Lincoln: University of Nebraska Press, 2018), Chap. 10, https://www.jstor.org/stable/j.ctvb1hrps.15.

23 George Cary Eggleston, *Red Eagle and the Wars with the Creek Indians of Alabama* (Gretna, LA: Pelican Publishing, 1999).

24 Eggleston, 13.

25 Frank L. Owsley, Jr. Prophet of War: Josiah Francis and the Creek War, *American Indian Quarterly*, Vol 9, (3), (Summer 1985), pp. 273–293.

26 Kokomoor, 331.

27 Ibid, 95.

28 Blackmon, 11.

29 Ibid, 12.

30 Kokomoor, 332.

31 Blackmon, 13.

32 Ibid, 13.

33 Ibid, 13.

34 Gregory Waskelov. *A Conquering Spirit: Fort Mims and the Red Stick War of 1813–1814.* (Alabama: University of Alabama Press, 2009), 99.

35 Waskelov, 99.

36 Braund, 25.

37 Kathryn Braund. *Tohopeka.* (USA: University of Kansas, 2011), 53.

38 Blackmon, 15.

39 Hickey, 148.

40 Blackmon, 21.

41 Ibid, 21.

42 Ibid, 21.

43 Hickey, 148.

44 Blackmon, 21–22.

45 Ibid, 21–22.

46 Ibid, 24.

47 Ibid, 24.

48 Ibid, 24.

49 Ibid, 25.

50 Ibid, 26–27.

51 Ibid, 36.

52 Kevin Kokomoor, *Of One Mind and Of One Government: The Rise and Fall of the Creek Nation in the Early Republic* (Lincoln: University of Nebraska Press, 2018), Cap. 10.

53 Dowd, 193.

54 R. David Edmunds, *Tecumseh and the Quest for Indian Leadership* (Boston: Little, Brown, 1984), 211.

Military History Chronicles • *Volume 2, Number 2* • *Fall 2025*

Manolis Bandouvas and the Interplay of Tradition, Resistance, and Allied Strategy in Crete During World War II

Emmanouil Peponas

NATO Defense College

Abstract

This article examines the dynamics of irregular guerrilla warfare in Crete during World War II, focusing on the operations of Manolis Bandouvas' band. Drawing on a wealth of primary sources and underexplored secondary materials, the study delves into the transformative stages of the Cretan resistance. First, it explores the formative years of German occupation (1941-1942), highlighting the emergence and consolidation of guerrilla bands, with particular emphasis on Bandouvas' strategic leadership. The core analysis centers on Bandouvas' pivotal operations in Simi and Viannos in 1943, assessing their tactical innovations and their impact on German counterinsurgency efforts. The final chapter addresses the concluding operations of Bandouvas' band (October 1943-October 1944), illustrating how the resistance adapted to evolving wartime conditions and external support dynamics, including Allied coordination.

Keywords: Crete, Greece, World War II, Bandouvas, Viannos, reprisals, war crimes, irregular warfare, occupation

Manolis Bandouvas y la interacción entre tradición, resistencia y estrategia aliada en Creta durante la Segunda Guerra Mundial

Resumen

Este artículo examina la dinámica de la guerra de guerrillas irregular en Creta durante la Segunda Guerra Mundial, centrándose en las operaciones de la banda de Manolis Bandouvas. Basándose en una gran cantidad de fuentes primarias y materiales secundarios poco explorados, el estudio profundiza en las etapas transformadoras de la resistencia cretense. En primer lugar, explora los años formativos de la ocupación alemana (1941-1942), destacando el sur-

doi: 10.18278/mhc.2.2.4

gimiento y la consolidación de las bandas guerrilleras, con especial énfasis en el liderazgo estratégico de Bandouvas. El análisis central se centra en las operaciones fundamentales de Bandouvas en Simi y Viannos en 1943, evaluando sus innovaciones tácticas y su impacto en los esfuerzos de contrainsurgencia alemanes. El capítulo final aborda las operaciones finales de la banda de Bandouvas (octubre de 1943-octubre de 1944), ilustrando cómo la resistencia se adaptó a las condiciones cambiantes de la guerra y la dinámica del apoyo externo, incluida la coordinación aliada.

Palabras clave: Creta, Grecia, Segunda Guerra Mundial, Bandouvas, Viannos, represalias, crímenes de guerra, guerra irregular, ocupación

二战期间的Manolis Bandouvas、以及克里特岛的传统、抵抗和盟军战略的相互作用

摘要

本文分析了二战期间克里特岛非正规游击战的动态，重点关注了Manolis Bandouvas的游击队行动。本研究利用大量一手资料和未被充分挖掘的次级资料，深入探讨了克里特岛抵抗运动的变革阶段。首先，本文探讨了德国占领的形成时期（1941-1942年），强调了游击队的出现和巩固，特别强调了Bandouvas的战略领导力。核心分析聚焦于1943年Bandouvas在锡米岛和维安诺斯的关键行动上，评估了他们的战术创新及其对德国反叛乱势力的影响。最后一章讨论了Bandouvas团伙的最后行动（1943年10月 – 1944年10月），阐明了抵抗运动如何适应不断变化的战时条件和外部支持动态，包括盟军的协调。

关键词：克里特岛，希腊，二战，Bandouvas，维安诺斯，报复，战争罪，非常规战争，占领

The Guerrilla Tradition in Crete

Crete is the largest island in Greece, consisting of four districts of 8,450² km. In 1940, 438,239 people lived there, mostly in the area's western and central parts.[1] Steep mountains characterize the Cretan geography: Lefka Ori in the Western and Mount Ida in the central part of the island are the highest, but—most importantly—the most dangerous for any army that hopes to control the region. Taking advantage of the forbidding ground, Cretans had developed a marvelous guerrilla tradition from the Renaissance Period. However, despite Venetians being the first to taste the skills of the local warriors, the latter excelled primarily against the Ottomans. Indeed, the presence of the High Porte's troops (1669–1913) combined with dozens of revolts against them. Those revolts and the continuous activity of guerrilla bands resulted in the Great Powers' decision to cede Crete to the Greek Kingdom in 1913.[2]

The evolution of local society was significantly influenced by the guerrilla warfare that occurred in the Cretan mountains against the Ottomans, mainly in the 19th century. First, the institution of the family became more important because it was used as a source of recruitment for guerrillas, and its wealth was necessary for the band's equipment.[3] In this context, as Crete, after the Greek Revolution (1821–1830), became a "war economy," the family's members began to be more willing to abandon the peaceful life and be guerrillas.[4]

Guerrilla tradition also affected the locals' connection to their arms. Even after the collapse of Ottoman domination, most of the men in Crete carried their guns in public ceremonies and did not doubt using them if they felt threatened. Simultaneously, the guerrilla warfare and the empowering of the family's role influenced the frequency of "vendetta," a bloody custom that still exists in Crete. The logic of

this tradition is simple— a man must take revenge for the murder of a family member. Thus, if a Turkish (and later a German) soldier had killed a guerrilla, his brothers were responsible for striking back and killing as many of their opponents as they could. For them, this was the only way to erase the family's shame. Understanding this tradition is crucial when analyzing operations like those conducted by Bandouvas during World War II.[5]

The Battle of Crete: The Praeludium of the Resistance Movement

By the late 1930s, the only formal military presence on the island was the V Infantry Division, consisting of approximately 20,000 highly trained Cretan soldiers commanded by Major General Georgios Papastergiou.[6] In October 1940, following the outbreak of the Greco-Italian War, the Greek dictator Ioannis Metaxas deployed the division to the front lines in Epirus, leaving Crete undefended.[7]

British troops began arriving on the island in November 1940 to compensate for the absence of Greek forces. These reinforcements, however, faced serious challenges: they suffered from communication difficulties and a lack of cohesive leadership, as their commander, Lieutenant General Bernard Freyberg, was unfamiliar with Crete's geography and had only been appointed in April 1941.[8]

The Battle of Crete ("Operation Mercury") commenced on 20 May 1941, following the German invasion of the Balkans, where they supported their Italian allies in their conflict with Greece. Despite six months of resistance, Greek forces could not halt the advancing Axis troops. The Greek V Division alone suffered 1,141 casualties, with thousands more injured, mirroring the losses across other units. After the Greek Army capitulated, its soldiers were prohibited from returning to Crete, as the Germans feared they would contribute to the island's defense. Consequently, many of these men ended up destitute on the streets of Athens and perished during the Great Famine of 1940–1941.[9]

On Crete, the unseasoned Commonwealth forces faced an elite German paratrooper assault, which began on 20 May. Although the local population, including women, children, and elders, intended to aid the British soldiers, they were largely unarmed. Compounding the Allies' difficulties, Freyberg or his superiors never ordered the destruction of the island's three airfields, leaving them vulnerable to German attacks. Indeed, while the Germans failed to capture the major airfields of Rethymno and Heraklion, they exploited a critical miscommunication among Allied forces in Maleme, western Crete. By dislodging the Maori defenders, German paratroopers gained control of the area and advanced eastward. Following this, Axis reinforcements arrived continuously, forcing the Allies to retreat, with assistance from the local population.[10] By early June, the battle had concluded, and Italian forces, coming from the Dodecanese, bloodlessly occupied the Lasithi region in eastern Crete.[11]

Despite the negative outcome of the battle for the Allies, the long guerrilla tradition of the locals did not dissipate with this defeat. Instead, it found new expression in resistance to the German occupation, as Cretan fighters once again took to the mountains to wage asymmetrical warfare against a foreign oppressor. This resistance culminated in notable operations such as the abduction of General Heinrich Kreipe in 1944 and played a pivotal role in undermining German control over the island.[12]

The First Years of the German Occupation, the Arrival of British Agents, and the Creation of Guerrilla Bands in Crete (1941–1942)

During the Battle of Crete, British intelligence operatives recruited several pro-Allied guerrilla leaders, including Antonis Grigorakis, known as "Satanas," Georgios Petrakis, or "Petrakogeorgis," and Manolis Bandouvas. Grigorakis, a former supporter of the influential statesman Eleftherios Venizelos, was arguably the most formidable of the three. However, his deteriorating health limited his involvement, and by the summer of 1942, he was compelled to leave the island.[13]

Thus, during the German Occupation (1941–1945), the resistance in Crete was primarily led by Petrakogeorgis and Bandouvas, alongside a few other less prominent local figures. Petrakogeorgis, a pro-British businessman with a pragmatic and calm demeanor,

Image 1: German paratroopers at the Battle of Crete (May 1941). Those elite forces faced the resistance of local irregular bands [Bundesarchiv].

had established himself as a key figure even before the war. In contrast, Bandouvas was more dynamic, ambitious, and forceful. Having served in the Greek Army during the Greco-Turkish War of 1919–1922 and later engaged in brigandage, by 1940, Bandouvas was a well-respected member of the local elite, known for both his wealth and integrity.[14]

Simultaneously, during the early years of the German occupation (1941–1942), British agents began arriving secretly in Crete. These men were often young military officers educated at prestigious institutions like Oxford and Cambridge, such as Christopher Montague Woodhouse, or adventurous mavericks like Patrick Leigh Fermor,

who thrived on breaking the rigid conventions of military discipline. Initially, their primary mission was to organize the escape of stranded Commonwealth soldiers with the help of local Cretans. However, the fierce desire of the Cretan population to resist the occupation soon prompted the development of more ambitious plans.[15]

On his part, Bandouvas, like many former guerrilla fighters, had refused to return to civilian life after the Battle of Crete. Thus, he gathered a group of men from villages in central Crete, equipping them with weapons he had hidden away. By late 1941, his efforts attracted the attention and support of British intelligence, who supplied him with additional arms, ammunition, and training. Bandouvas organized and disciplined his force with British assistance, which expanded rapidly.[16] He also attempted to collaborate with communist guerrillas in western Crete, whose influence was growing under the leadership of figures such as Major General Manolis Mandakas, a pro-Venizelist who later aligned with the Greek Communist Party (Kommounistiko Komma Elladas, KKE).[17]

The British, however, viewed such alliances with suspicion. Their primary concern was that the Greek Communist Party might leverage the resistance movement to seize power after the liberation of Greece. This concern created tensions between British agents and Bandouvas. Besides, while Bandouvas favored bold and rapid offensives aimed at forcing a German withdrawal from Crete, the British pursued a more calculated approach. Their strategy prioritized smaller-scale ambushes designed to inflict steady attrition on German forces, aligning with broader Allied plans to stretch Axis resources thin across multiple fronts.

In this context, 1942 proved pivotal for the development of Cretan resistance. This year, Bandouvas' and Petrakogeorgis' forces clashed with German troops on several occasions, solidifying their control over the central Cretan mountains. However, tensions between Bandouvas and British operatives grew, primarily because their actions often triggered harsh German reprisals. These reprisals deepened the locals' hatred of the Germans, they also fueled resentment toward the British

for provoking such suffering. Additionally, the British could not provide the support Bandouvas demanded and frequently favored Petrakogeorgis, which triggered the Cretan leader.[18]

Meanwhile, communist factions continued to strengthen their presence in Crete and attempted to ally with Bandouvas. While their efforts were limited to temporarily embedding one of their comrades, Yanni Podias, in Bandouvas' group, these internal rivalries, complicated alliances with foreign agents, and the rising influence of the communist forces contributed to a fractured resistance movement. These dynamics would profoundly shape the course of the struggle in Crete in 1943.

Bandouvas and Operation Albumen (1942–1943)

In the summer of 1942, the Allies launched a series of commando operations in Crete under the codename "Albumen." These missions targeted the strategic airfields of Heraklion, Maleme, Tymbaki, and Kastelli, which the Germans used as transit hubs for transporting supplies to North Africa. The significance of these airfields in sustaining Axis forces in Egypt made them a high priority for British planners.[19]

The first attacks of 1942 successfully destroyed several Luftwaffe aircraft at Heraklion and Kastelli and resulted in the deaths of several German soldiers. The Allied focus on Cretan airfields continued into 1943, with renewed operations designed to damage German capabilities and mislead the Axis into believing that an Allied invasion of Crete was imminent. This deception aligned with broader Allied strategies in the Mediterranean, particularly to divert German resources from Sicily, where the real invasion (Operation Husky) was planned. The sabotage missions aimed to inflict heavy casualties on Axis forces and prevent the German aircraft stationed in Crete from interfering in the Sicily campaign.[20]

On 23 June 1943, a team of saboteurs landed at Tripiti Beach in southern Crete to execute the operation. The group included several well-trained Cretans—Kimon Zografakis, Yannis Androulakis, and Giorgis Voskakis—who had been trained in Egypt and possessed intimate knowledge of the terrain. The operation's leader, British Colonel David Sutherland, divided his team into three groups: the first group, led by Lieutenant Anders Larsen, targeted the Kastelli airfield, the second group, under Lieutenant Kenneth Lamonby, focused on the Heraklion airfield, and the third group, led by Lieutenant Rony Rovs, aimed to sabotage the Tymbaki airfield.[21]

While the groups targeting Heraklion and Tymbaki achieved limited success due to the Germans having moved their aircraft to more secure locations, the operation at Kastelli was more effective. Larsen's group managed to distract the Germans on the western side of the airfield, allowing other commandos to infiltrate from the east. They destroyed aircraft and ammunition dumps, delivering a significant blow to

German operations in the area. However, the escape phase proved challenging. After completing their mission, the commandos regrouped at Tripiti, intending to leave Crete by boat. On 10 July 1943, the Germans discovered their location, resulting in a fierce battle in which Lamonby was killed.[22]

Manolis Bandouvas and his guerrillas played a critical role in supporting Operation Albumen. Their most significant contributions occurred in Kastelli, where Yannis Bandouvas, Manolis' brother, directly participated in the operation. The guerrillas engaged German forces, provided logistical support, such as food and supplies, and guided the saboteurs through the rugged terrain to their targets. These contributions were vital to the operation's success and demonstrated the close cooperation between the Cretan resistance and Allied forces.[23]

However, these successes came at a high cost: Axis forces retaliated by executing 62 civilians near Heraklion, highlighting the brutal consequences of resistance operations on the local population.[24] Besides, for Manolis Bandouvas, such sabotage missions were not enough. Convinced that an Allied invasion of Crete was imminent, he envisioned a large-scale confrontation with Axis forces. His determination to prepare for such an operation ultimately led to the tragic events of the Viannos massacre, one of the most devastating German reprisals of World War II.

Image 2: Manolis Bandouvas (center) with his brothers, Yiannis and Nikos, who also participated in the resistance movement against the Germans. Family connections were crucial for the Cretan guerrillas [Creta One].

Bandouvas' Operations in Simi and Viannos (1943)

In the summer of 1943, according to British agent Patrick Leigh Fermor, Manolis Bandouvas led a seasoned guerrilla force of approximately 160 men. This group was composed of a diverse array of individuals, including New Zealand and Australian soldiers who had fought in the Battle of Crete, a former Russian prisoner, students, elders, a small contingent of communist fighters, a larger group of royalists, pro-Venizelist military officers, and mostly illiterate villagers like Bandouvas himself. At this time, Bandouvas claimed that if he had sufficient arms, he could recruit over 2,000 additional fighters.[25]

Bandouvas' ambitions were clear—assisting British commandos in clandestine operations and organizing ambushes against the Germans was insufficient. He sought to liberate Crete outright. The Germans' confiscation of his fortune in the spring of 1943 and the execution of several of his family members only intensified his resolve. By the summer of 1943, with rumors of an Allied invasion of Italy and potentially Crete, Bandouvas was determined to take decisive action.[26]

In retrospect, Bandouvas' decisions can appear reckless. Still, it is essential to understand the context of 1943—the information available to Cretan guerrillas was often vague, and Bandouvas lacked the formal education of a military officer or diplomat. His worldview was shaped by traditional values, where every man was seen as a potential warrior, and honor, or "timi," was paramount. For people like Bandouvas, defending personal and family honor precedes the broader strategic consequences. These cultural factors heavily influenced his subsequent actions.

In addition to these cultural and personal motivations, Bandouvas had practical concerns in the summer of 1943. His relations with the British had soured due to his persistent demands for more weapons. Meanwhile, Petrakogeorgis in central Crete and communist guerrilla bands in the west were growing stronger, challenging his leadership. Thus when Bandouvas learned of the imminent Italian withdrawal from the island, he interpreted it as a sign that an Allied invasion of Crete was near and felt compelled to act swiftly.[27]

Between 10 and 15 August 1943, Bandouvas mobilized as many fighters as possible, claiming his forces swelled to 3,222 guerrillas. Most came from the Viannos region in central Crete and were bound to Bandouvas through family or economic ties.[28] Their motivations were a mix of rage, patriotism, and honor, particularly as many had lost family members to German reprisals. The vendetta culture, deeply ingrained in Cretan society, played a key role in driving these men to fight, often with the expectation of sacrificing their lives for the cause.[29]

Bandouvas, whose own family had suffered from German atrocities, believed he could liberate central Crete before the anticipated Allied invasion.[30] However, no British agents supported his plan; Patrick Leigh Fermor secretly worked on extracting the commander of the Italian 51st Infantry Division, "Siena," Angelo Carta, from the island to Egypt. Carta, a royalist who resisted German orders to execute civilians, had expressed a desire to collaborate with the Allies. Fermor's operations had to remain covert to avoid alerting the Germans.[31]

Unaware of these British plans and fixated on his belief in an imminent invasion, Bandouvas attacked a small German garrison in Simi on 9-10 September 1943. The timing was significant—Italy had capitulated to the Allies on 8 September, and the guerrilla leader assumed Crete would be next. The operation resulted in the deaths of two Axis soldiers but also alerted the Germans, precisely the outcome the British had feared.[32]

Following the attack on Simi, Bandouvas' forces moved to Viannos, a hub of armed resistance. He deployed approximately 300 guerrillas, and on 12 September, a German convoy advanced against them. In the initial skirmish between Simi and Pefko villages, the Greeks emerged victorious, capturing hostages and spoils. Bandouvas then ordered ambushes to be prepared in case German reinforcements arrived from Chania.[33]

Bandouvas led his men to Agio Pnevma to further consolidate his position and recruited additional fighters from nearby villages. He also moved to Selekano, where thousands of Italian soldiers, eager to surrender, had gathered. He disarmed them and invited any willing soldiers to join his forces. According to Bandouvas, 360 Italians agreed to fight alongside him, though even this number proved insufficient for his ambitious plans.[34]

On his behalf, Lieutenant General Friedrich-Wilhelm Müller, the German commander of "Fortress Crete," had no intention of allowing the mass surrender of his former Italian allies to the guerrillas or permitting the resistance to dominate central Crete. To suppress the growing insurgency, Müller dispatched 2,000 troops to Viannos and surrounding villages, with brutal instructions:

> *Destroy the Viannos province. Execute immediately, without trial, every man over 16 years old and anyone captured in the countryside, regardless of gender or age.*[35]

Indeed, following Müller's orders, German forces encircled Viannos. On 13 September 1943, they entered the village of Agios Vasileios and ordered the residents to remain indoors, warning that those who disobeyed would be executed. This tactic was designed to prevent civilians from escaping, a method the Germans would use repeatedly in the coming days.[36]

The following day, German troops set fire to the villages of Pefko and Simi, near the site of the recent battles. Simultaneously, they destroyed several other villages—Kefalovrisi, Kato Simi, Amiras, Vahos, Agios, Mirtos, Gdohia, Riza, Mournies, Mithi, Malles, Christos, and Metaxohori. Hundreds of civilians, especially men over 16, were executed in a calculated wave of terror. For the German soldiers, the atrocities became a grotesque celebration; they danced, sang, and mocked the grieving survivors.[37]

In response, Bandouvas' forces managed to kill over 20 German soldiers but stood little chance of halting the overwhelming enemy. The terror unleashed by the Germans also hampered guerrilla recruitment efforts, as fear spread throughout the local population.[38] On their part, the German occupation forces imprisoned around 300 hostages in Ano Viannos' high school, threatening to execute them unless Bandouvas released the German soldiers he had captured. Realizing the situation was hopeless, the Cretan leader was compelled to comply with the German demands, releasing the prisoners. However, this did not pacify the Germans, who, on 14 October, razed the villages of Kefalovrisi, Krevvatia, Pefko, Simi, Kalami, Sikologos, Mirtos, Gdohia, Mournies, and Kaimeno.[39]

On 15 September, Bandouvas' forces began a five-day retreat, aiming to evade the German troops by moving towards Sfakia, about 150 kilometers west of Viannos. Thus, the guerrillas passed near Kastelli airport, some 35 kilometers south of Heraklion, traveling by night to avoid detection. Though most of the group reached safety, a small contingent lost its way and was forced into battle near Omalos Mountain. Both sides sustained heavy casualties during this skirmish, marking a tragic and bloody chapter in the Cretan resistance.[40]

In the aftermath of the war, historians debated Bandouvas' motivations. A central point of contention is the theory that specific British agents may have encouraged Bandouvas to act to divert German attention to a secondary front. However, the archival evidence does not conclusively support this hypothesis, and figures such as Patrick Leigh Fermor were quick to express their dissent regarding this interpretation.

Regarding the German response, it is more plausible that they utilized Bandouvas' actions as a pretext to rationalize their brutal reprisals. Viannos had long served as a bastion for Cretan guerrillas and British agents, which alarmed the German occupiers, including Lieutenant General Müller. The destruction of this region served the objective of instilling fear within the local population and temporarily suppressing guerrilla activities. The memory of

these atrocities persists in the collective consciousness of the local community, with a small museum dedicated to commemorating the events and honoring the victims.

The Last Operations of Bandouvas' band in Crete (October 1943–October 1944)

Following the Viannos operation, Bandouvas faced immense pressure from German forces. His attempts to escape from Crete were fraught with danger, as German troops had encircled his hideouts and executed several members of his family. These developments forced him into hiding in the rugged mountains of Sfakia, where he remained for approximately a month. Despite the challenges, he escaped with a small group of companions aboard a British vessel on 31 October 1943. Their destination was Egypt, where Bandouvas and his comrades were exiled for over a year.[41]

On 17 November 1943, the Germans issued an appeal to the Cretan population, stating the following:

The arch-brigand Bandouvas has abandoned the island with his bodyguards. Thus, Crete has been freed from this treacherous individual who caused so much suffering to the peaceful population. If so many women are widowed and so many children are orphaned, it is because of this criminal. The fight against the remnants of his gang continues with relentless cruelty.

(...) The German Army is a friend of the Cretan people. It will not allow this beautiful island to become a theater of war again or a haven for the disturbing activities of the gangs—these enemies of the people.

Everyone who provides assistance to the army during this struggle will be welcomed.[42]

After Bandouvas' departure, his unit's activities significantly diminished. Some members continued operating under the leadership of his brother, Yannis Bandouvas, but their capacity was limited. Although sporadic ambushes against German forces and executions of suspected collaborators persisted, the unit's influence had waned by 1944. The peak of their operational power and influence was clearly over.[43]

Manolis Bandouvas returned to Crete on 9 October 1944, at a time when German control had significantly weakened due to the Axis' defeats on both the western and eastern fronts. Upon his return, he immediately resumed command of his band and, on 11 October, issued an ultimatum to the German commander of the island, General Hans-Georg Benthack, who was surrounded in Heraklion. In the ultimatum, Bandouvas warned the German forces that his men were prepared to launch an attack if they did not abandon the city. Tensions were high, as hundreds of guerrillas were eager to exact bloody revenge on an enemy responsible for numerous atrocities against their families.[44]

Recognizing the precariousness of his position, Benthack arranged a meeting with Bandouvas, mediated by the Vicar of the Holy Metropolis of Crete, Evgenios Psallodakis. During the negotiations, the German commander agreed to surrender Heraklion without a fight to spare his troops from potential reprisals. Following the agreement, Bandouvas entered the city as a liberator and assumed the role of Military Commander of the region, tasked with restoring security and order in the Heraklion Prefecture. This pivotal act marked the end of the occupation in the area and solidified Bandouvas' legacy as one of Crete's most prominent and respected resistance leaders.[45]

Conclusion

The Cretan resistance movement during World War II exemplified a distinctive model of irregular warfare, deeply rooted in the island's rugged terrain, its population's historical proclivity for guerrilla tactics, and the intertwining of traditional values with modern resistance strategies. The operations of Manolis Bandouvas' band illustrate these defining characteristics, showcasing how localized agency, cultural imperatives, and external influences converged to shape the resistance's trajectory.

Bandouvas' leadership reflected both the strengths and limitations of the Cretan approach to asymmetrical warfare. His ability to mobilize a diverse force, including villagers, escaped Allied soldiers, and former Italian troops, demonstrated the adaptability and re-

Image 3: Viannos is a small village in Crete today. The collective memory
of the German war crimes is still active [Agonas tis Kritis].

sourcefulness emblematic of Cretan resistance leaders. Equally significant was his cultural alignment with the ethos of "timi" (honor), which motivated both his personal commitment and the resolve of his fighters. These factors reinforced the moral and psychological dimensions of the resistance, enabling it to persist despite severe reprisals and logistical constraints.

At the operational level, Bandouvas' actions underscored the dual role of resistance fighters as both military and political actors. While demonstrating tactical ingenuity, his confrontations with German forces in Simi and Viannos also drew attention to the challenges of balancing local imperatives with broader strategic objectives. These operations, characterized by ambushes and the integration of captured resources, highlighted the guerrilla movement's reliance on initiative and decentralized command structures. However, the devastating German reprisals following these engagements revealed the inherent risks of confrontation and underscored the tension between local ambitions and Allied strategic priorities.

Bandouvas' contributions to the resistance resonate within the broader context of irregular warfare. His actions exemplify the importance of integrating cultural and local knowledge into guerrilla operations, a principle that continues to inform modern counterinsurgency doctrines. Moreover, his efforts emphasized the centrality of leadership in sustaining morale and cohesion within diverse and often fractious resistance movements.

As the historiography of World War II continues to evolve, the study of figures like Bandouvas offers valuable insights into the dynamics of resistance under occupation. By examining his legacy, we gain a deeper understanding of how local actors shaped the course of military resistance, navigating the interplay between traditional values, immediate wartime exigencies, and the shifting tides of global conflict. In this context, Bandouvas' band symbolized the indomitable spirit of the Cretan resistance and contributed a critical chapter to the broader narrative of irregular warfare in the 20th century.

About the Author

Emmanouil (Manolis) Peponas holds a PhD in Modern and Contemporary Greek History from the National and Kapodistrian University of Athens, an MA in Modern and Contemporary History from the University of Ioannina, and a BA degree in History and Philosophy. He is a Junior Associate Fellow at the NATO Defense College and an Adjunct Instructor at the University of the People. He has authored numerous publications on military and diplomatic history and has received prestigious awards, including the Ryoichi Sasakawa Young Leaders Fellowship.

References

Primary Sources and Newspapers

Πληθυσμός της Ελλάδας κατά την απογραφήν της 16 Οκτωβρίου 1940 [Population of Greece during the census of 16 October 1940], National Print Shop, Athens 1946.

Πληθυσμός της Ελλάδας κατά την απογραφήν της 7 Απριλίου 1951 [Population of Greece during the census of 7 April 1951], National Print Shop, Athens 1955.

Empros, n. 684, 21-5-1947.

Hellenic Army History Directorate, Emmanouil Bandouvas' report about the Cretan National Resistance, 20-8-1945.

Hellenic Army History Directorate, Announcement of German Commander of Crete regarding Bandouvas, 17-11-1943.

Kazantzakis, Nikos. Kalitsounakis, Ioannis. Kakridis, Ioannis (1983). *Έκθεσις της Κεντρικής Επιτροπής Διαπιστώσεως Ωμοτήτων εν Κρήτη [Report of the Central Committee for the Determination of Atrocities in Crete]*, Heraklion: Municipality of Heraklion.

Rizospastis, n. 10.082, 3-6-1947.

Rizospastis, n. 10.105, 29-7-1947.

Rizospastis, n. 10.113, 9-8-1947.

Sanoudakis, Antonis (1979). *Καπετάν Μπαντουβά Απομνημονεύματα [Captain Bandouvas' Memoirs],* Athens: Knossos.

WO 373/46/22, Recommendation for Award for The Earl of Jellicoe Rank, 5 November 1942.

Bibliography

"Μπαντουβάς Ι. Κωνσταντίνος." [Bandouvas I. Konstantinos] *Vouli Watch,* n.d., https://vouliwatch.gr/mp/mpantoyvas-konstantinos.

"Mr. Churchill's Statements on the Fighting in Crete." *Bulletin of International News,* vol. 18, no. 11, 1941.

"Müller, Friedrich-Wilhelm (1897–1947)." *Gedenkorte Europa,* n.d. https://www.gedenkorte-europa.eu/de_de/article-muller-friedrich-wilhelm-1897-1947.html.

Allbaugh, Leland G. "The Cretan Family." *Crete,* Princeton: Princeton University Press, 1953.

Antonakos, Sarantis. "Το αντιμεταξικό κίνημα στα Χανιά το 1938." [The anti-Metaxas movement in Chania in 1938] *Istoria Ikonografimeni,* vol. 197, November 1984.

Beevor, Anthony. *Crete. The Battle and the Resistance.* London: Murray, 2005.

Brewer, David. *Greece, the Decade at War. Occupation, Resistance and Civil War,* p. 53. London: I. B. Tauris, 2016.

Broers, Michael. "Revolution As Vendetta: Napoleonic Piedmont 1801-1814 II." *The Historical Journal,* vol. 33, no. 4, 1990.

Brögger, Jan. "Conflict Resolution and the Role of the Bandit in Peasant Society." *Anthropological Quarterly,* vol. 41, no. 4, 1968.

Cassia, Paul Sant. "Banditry, Myth, and Terror in Cyprus and Other Mediterranean Societies." *Comparative Studies in Society and History,* vol. 35, no. 4, 1993.

Cavallar, Osvaldo; Kirshner, Julius. "Vendetta." *Jurists and Jurisprudence in Medieval Italy: Texts and Contexts,* University of Toronto Press, 2020.

Clark, Mark Edmond. "The German Invasion of Crete and the Importance of Intelligence and Logistical Planning in the Rapid Deployment of Light Units." *Army History*, no. 21, 1991.

Dean, Trevor. "Marriage and Mutilation: Vendetta in Late Medieval Italy." *Past & Present*, no. 157, 1997.

Fielding, Xan. *Hide and Seek: The Story of a War-time Agent.* London: Secker & Warburg, 1954.

Galbraith, James K. "The War Economy." *Archives of the Levy Economics Institute*, 2001, 71. https://digitalcommons.bard.edu/levy_archives/71.

Gatchel, Theodore L. "Can a Battle Be Lost in the Mind of the Commander?" *Naval War College Review*, vol. 38, no. 1, 1985.

Gordon, N. P. J. "The Murder of Buondelmonte: Contesting Place in Early Fourteenth-Century Florentine Chronicles." *Renaissance Studies*, vol. 20, no. 4, 2006.

Greene, Molly. "Between Wine and Olive Oil." *A Shared World: Christians and Muslims in the Early Modern Mediterranean.* Princeton University Press, 2000.

Holland, James. *Sicily '43: The First Assault on Fortress Europe.* New York: Grove Atlantic, 2020.

Jones, Barry. "Freyberg, Bernard Cyril." *Dictionary of World Biography*, 8th ed., Canberra: ANU Press, 2021.

Kallivretakis, Leonidas. "A Century of Revolutions: The Cretan Question between European and Near Eastern Politics" in Paschalis M. Kitromilides (ed.), *Eleftherios Venizelos: The Trials of Statesmanship*. Edinburgh: Edinburgh University Press, 2006.

Kalogerakis, Giorgos. "Εκδήλωση μνήμης – Ομάδες Μπαντουβάδων" [Commemorative event – Banduvas' groups], *Patris*, 29-9-2008, https://archive.patris.gr/articles/142249.

Kallogerakis, Giorgos. "Το α' σαμποτάζ του αεροδρομίου Καστελίου και ο καπετάν Μανόλης Μπαντουβάς" [The first sabotage in Kastelli airfield and the captain Manolis Bandouvas]. *Patris*, 24-12-2008, https://archive.patris.gr/articles/148156.

Kallogerakis, Giorgos. "62 Μάρτυρες" [62 Martyrs]. *Patris*, 15-7-2020, https://www.patris.gr/istoria/62-martyres-ioannis-emm-manoysakis-14-ioynioy-1942/#:~:text=%CE%A4%CE%BF%20%CF%83%CE%B1%CE%BC%CF%80%CE%BF%CF%84%CE%AC%CE%B6%20%CF%84%C

E%BF%CF%85%20%CE%B1%CE%B5%CF%81%CE%BF%CE%B
4%CF%81%CE%BF%CE%BC%CE%AF%CE%BF%CF%85%20
%CE%97%CF%81%CE%B1%CE%BA%CE%BB%CE%B5%CE%AF%CE%B
F%CF%85,12%20%CF%80%CE%B1%CF%84%CF%81%CE%B9%CF
%8E%CF%84%CE%B5%CF%82%20%CF%84%CE%B7%CF%82%20
3%CE%B7%CF%82%20%CE%99%CE%BF%CF%85%CE%B
D%CE%AF%CE%BF%CF%85.

Kontakis, Ioannis. "Η μαρτυρία του Γιάννη Κοντάκη για τα γεγονότα της Βιάννου" [The testimony of Yannis Kontakis about the events of Viannos]. *Patris*, 29-4-2005, https://archive.patris.gr/articles/59484.

Koukounas, Dimosthenis. *Η Εθνική Αντίσταση στην Κρήτη 1941-1945 [The National Resistance in Crete 1941-1945]*. Athens: Historia, 2022.

Kressel, Gideon M., et al. "Sororicide/Filiacide: Homicide for Family Honour [and Comments and Reply]." *Current Anthropology*, vol. 22, no. 2, 1981.

M. E. P. "Greece and the War." *Bulletin of International News*, vol. 21, no. 3, 1944.

Magoulios George; Maniadis Metaxas Georgios. "The Expansion of the Contemporary Economic Role of Crete throughout Its Extensive History." *International Journal of Economics, Business and Management Studies*, vol. 4, no. 1, 2017.

Magrini, Tullia. "Manhood and Music in Western Crete: Contemplating Death." *Ethnomusicology*, vol. 44, no. 3, 2000.

Maravelakis, Iosif P. "'Unofficial Duties' in Periods of Crisis during the 1866–69 Revolt: The Cases of Charles Dickson and Lysimachus Calocherino." *From Crete to London: An Example of a Bottom-up Exercise of British Power in the 19th Century Ottoman Empire*, Wiesbaden: Harrassowitz Verlag, 2024.

Moorey, Chris. "Ottoman Rule II: 1821 to 1898." *A History of Crete*, Cotton Row: Haus Publishing, 2019.

N.A. *Ιστορία της 5ης ΤΑΞΠΖ "V Μεραρχία Κρητών" [History of the 5th Infantry Brigade "V Cretan Division"]*. Rethymno: Military Museum of Rethymno, 2014.

Patira Edwards, Ngāpuhi (1919–2005), interviewed by Megan Hutching, 27 November 2000, for the *Second World War oral history project – Crete*. From the collections of the Alexander Turnbull Library Oral History and Sound collection, OHInt-0729-08, n.d., https://www.28maoribattalion.org.nz/audio/patira-edwards -describes-being-fed-cretan-people.

Saab, Ann Pottinger. "The Doctors' Dilemma: Britain and the Cretan Crisis 1866-

69." *The Journal of Modern History*, vol. 49, no. 4, 1977.

Skalidakis, Jannis. *Η Κρήτη στα χρόνια της Κατοχής 1941–1945 [Crete in the years of Occupation 1941-1945]*. Athens: Asini, 2023.

Stratakis, Giorgos. *Ο Γολγοθάς της 5ης Μεραρχίας Κρητών 1940–1941 [The Calvary of the 5th Cretan Division 1940–1941]*. Athens: Svoura, 2024.

Stroud, Rick. *Kidnap in Crete: The True Story of the Abduction of a Nazi General*, London: Bloomsbury, 2015.

Notes

1   *Πληθυσμός της Ελλάδας κατά την απογραφήν της 16 Οκτωβρίου 1940 [Population of Greece during the census of 16 October 1940]* (Athens: National Print Shop, 1946), 10-12.

2   Paschalis M. Kitromilides, "Crete" in Paschalis M. Kitromilides and Constantinos Tsoukalas (ed.) *The Greek Revolution: A Critical Dictionary* (Harvard: Harvard University Press, 2021), 193-202; Ann Pottinger Saab, "The Doctors' Dilemma: Britain and the Cretan Crisis 1866-69." *The Journal of Modern History* 49 (4) (1977): D1383-407; Iosif P. Maravelakis, "'Unofficial Duties in Periods of Crisis during the 1866–69 Revolt: The Cases of Charles Dickson and Lysimachus Calocherino." *From Crete to London: An Example of a Bottom-up Exercise of British Power in the 19th Century Ottoman Empire* (Leipzig: Harrassowitz Verlag, 2024), 85-106; Chris Moorey, "Ottoman Rule II: 1821 to 1898." *A History of Crete* (London: Haus Publishing, 2019), 184-224; Leonidas Kallivretakis, "A Century of Revolutions: The Cretan Question between European and Near Eastern Politics" in Paschalis M. Kitromilides (ed.). *Eleftherios Venizelos: The Trials of Statesmanship* (Edinburgh: Edinburgh University Press, 2006), 11-35.

3   Leland G. Allbaugh, "The Cretan Family," *Crete* (Princeton: Princeton University Press, 1953), 73-96.

4   James K. Galbraith, "The War Economy." *Archives of the Levy Economics Institute.* 71, (2001), https://digitalcommons.bard.edu/levy_archives/71. Retrieved on 2-9-2024.

5   Paul Sant Cassia, "Banditry, Myth, and Terror in Cyprus and Other Mediterranean Societies." *Comparative Studies in Society and History* 35 (4), (1993): 773-95; Gideon M. Kressel, et al. "Sororicide/Filiacide: Homicide for Family Honour [and Comments and Reply]." *Current Anthropology* 22 (2), (1981): 141-58; Jan Brögger, "Conflict Resolution and the Role of the Bandit in Peasant Society." *Anthropological Quarterly* 41 (4), (1968): 228-240; Osvaldo Cavallar and Julius Kirshner "Vendetta." *Jurists and Jurisprudence in Medieval Italy: Texts and Contexts* (Toronto: University of Toronto Press, 2020), 422-431; Tullia Magrini, "Manhood and Music in Western Crete: Contemplating Death." *Ethnomusicology* 44 (3), (2000): 432-433.

According to the word's etymology and the fact that the phenomenon had been witnessed in several Italian cities, Vendetta probably has Italian origins. See (selectively): N. P. J. Gordon, "The Murder of Buondelmonte: Contesting Place in Early Fourteenth-Century Florentine Chronicles." *Renaissance Studies* 20 (4) (2006): 459-477; Michael Broers, "Revolution as Vendetta: Napoleonic Piedmont 1801–1814 II." *The Historical Journal* 33 (4) (1990): 787–809; Trevor Dean, "Marriage and Mutilation: Vendetta in Late Medieval Italy." *Past & Present* 157 (1997): 3'36.

6   *Ιστορία της 5ης ΤΑΞΠΖ "V Μεραρχία Κρητών" [History of the 5th Infantry Brigade "V Cretan Division"],* (Rethymno: Military Museum of Rethymno, 2014), 88.

7   *Ibid,* 88-92.

8   Barry Jones, "Freyberg, Bernard Cyril," *Dictionary of World Biography* (Canberra: ANU Press, 2021), 328.

9   Giorgos Stratakis, *Ο Γολγοθάς της 5ης Μεραρχίας Κρητών 1940-1941 [The Calvary of the 5th Cretan Division 1940–1941]* (Athens: Svoura, 2024).

10 Patira Edwards, Ngāpuhi (1919-2005), interviewed by Megan Hutching, 27 November 2000, for the *Second World War oral history project – Crete.* From the collections of the Alexander Turnbull Library Oral History and Sound collection, OHInt-0729-08, n.d., https://www.28maoribattalion.org.nz/audio/patira-edwards-describes-being-fed-cretan-people. Retrieved on 13 September 2024.

11 Theodore L. Gatchel, "Can a Battle Be Lost in the Mind of the Commander?" *Naval War College Review,* 38 (1) (1985): 96-99; Mark Edmond Clark, "The German Invasion of Crete and the Importance of Intelligence and Logistical Planning in the Rapid Deployment of Light Units." *Army History,* 21 (1991): 31-36; M. E. P. "Greece and the War." *Bulletin of International News,* 21 (3) (1944): 91-101.

Churchill stated during the Battle of Crete: "It is a most strange and grim battle that is being fought. Our side have no air support because they have no aerodromes, not because they have no aeroplanes. The other side have very little or none of artillery and tanks. Neither side has any means of retreat." See "Mr. Churchill's Statements on the Fighting in Crete." *Bulletin of International News,* 18 (11) (1941): 690-691. The above statement is partly false, because airdromes existed, but only the Germans took advantage of them.

12 David Brewer, *Greece, the Decade at War. Occupation, Resistance and Civil War* (London: I. B. Tauris, 2016), 53.

13 Anthony Beevor, *Crete. The Battle and the Resistance* (London: Murray, 2005), 51.

14 Xan Fielding, *Hide and Seek: The Story of a War-time Agent* (London: Secker & Warburg, 1954), 194; Dimosthenis Koukounas, *Η Εθνική Αντίσταση στην Κρήτη 1941–1945 [The National Resistance in Crete 1941–1945]* (Athens: Historia, 2022), 28.

According to Chris Woodhouse, a British agent who served in Crete and mainland Greece, and later became a successful academic, everyone trusted Bandouvas' integrity and skills. This led him to provide significant amounts of supplies to the Cretan guerrilla leader. However, the relationships between them would deteriorate after some years.

15 Beevor, *Op. Cit.*, p. 130.

16 Hellenic Army History Directorate, Emmanouil Bandouvas' report about the Cretan National Resistance, 20/8/1945.

17 Koukounas, *Ibid,* 28-31.

18 As historian Antony Beevor insightfully observed, Petrakogeorgis was Bandouvas' "frere ennemi" (brother-enemy). Beevor, *Op. Cit.*, 127.

19 WO 373/46/22, Recommendation for Award for The Earl of Jellicoe Rank, 5 November 1942.

20 James Holland, *Sicily '43: The First Assault on Fortress Europe* (New York: Grove Atlantic, 2020).

21 Giorgos Kallogerakis, "Το α' σαμποτάζ του αεροδρομίου Καστελίου και ο καπετάν Μανόλης Μπαντουβάς" [The first sabotage in Kastelli airfield and the captain Manolis Bandouvas], *Patris,* 24/12/2008, https://archive.patris.gr/articles/148156.

22 Ibid.

23 Giorgos Kallogerakis, "62 Μάρτυρες" [62 Martyrs], *Patris,* 15/7/2020, https://www.patris.gr/istoria/62-martyres-ioannis-emm-manoysakis-14-ioyn ioy-1942/#:~:text=%CE%A4%CE%BF%20%CF%83%CE%B1%CE%B C%CF%80%CE%BF%CF%84%CE%AC%CE%B6%20%CF%84%C E%BF%CF%85%20%CE%B1%CE%B5%CF%81%CE%BF%CE%B 4%CF%81%CE%BF%CE%BC%CE%AF%CE%BF%CF%85%20 %CE%97%CF%81%CE%B1%CE%BA%CE%BB%CE%B5%CE%B F%CF%85,12%20%CF%80%CE%B1%CF%84%CF%81%CE%B9%CF %8E%CF%84%CE%B5%CF%82%20%CF%84%CE%B7%CF%82%20 3%CE%B7%CF%82%20%CE%99%CE%BF%CF%85%CE%B D%CE%AF%CE%BF%CF%85.

24 Hellenic Army History Directorate, Emmanouil Bandouvas' report about the Cretan National Resistance, 20-8-1945.

25 *Ibid*, 149.

26 Giorgos Kalogerakis, "Εκδήλωση μνήμης – Ομάδες Μπαντουβάδων" ["Commemorative event – Banduvas' groups"], *Patris,* 29-9-2008, https://archive.patris.gr/arti cles/142249. Retrieved on 10-9-2024.

27 Koukounas, *Op. Cit.,* 42-44.

28 Antonis Sanoudakis, *Καπετάν Μπαντουβά Απομνημονεύματα [Captain Bandouvas' Memoirs]* (Athens: Knossos, 1979), 317.

29 German atrocities in Crete began already in July of 1941 and included executions of civilians in Kontomari, Kandanos, and several other villages. For their behavior, see:

Jannis Skalidakis, *Η Κρήτη στα χρόνια της Κατοχής 1941–1945 [Crete in the years of Occupation 1941–1945]* (Athens: Asini, 2023).

30 According to the retired Colonel and guerrilla leader Ioannis Kontakis, Bandouvas desired to face the Germans in a large-scale battle in July 1943. However, Kontakis himself insisted that such a confrontation could provoke serious retaliations by the occupants and the destruction of Viannos. The same officer narrated that Bandouvas was frustrated and threatened to kill him, but finally agreed to postpone his plans.

See: Ioannis Kontakis, "Η μαρτυρία του Γιάννη Κοντάκη για τα γεγονότα της Βιάννου" [The testimony of Yannis Kontakis about the events of Viannos], *Patris,* 29-4-2005, https://archive.patris.gr/articles/59484. Retrieved on 10-9-2024.

31 Beevor, *Op. Cit.,* 150.

32 Sanoudakis, *Op. Cit.,* 318-319.

33 *Ibid,* 319-322.

34 *Ibid,* 322-324.

35 Rick Stroud, *Kidnap in Crete: The True Story of the Abduction of a Nazi General* (London: Bloomsbury, 2015), 92.

36 Beevor, *Op. Cit.,* 151.

37 In 1945, the Greek government tasked renowned intellectuals Nikos Kazantzakis, Ioannis Kakridis, and Ioannis Kalitsounakis with investigating German war crimes in Crete. Kazantzakis, born in Heraklion in 1883, and his colleagues focused their report on the September 1943 massacres in Viannos. They described the German occupation forces' behavior in Amiras in particularly chilling detail:

"When the Germans entered Amiras, the locals, following their mayor's advice, greeted them at the village entrance with wine, raki, and food. The Germans, having surrounded the area, captured all the men—around 100—and executed them by the roadside without trial. The executions took place in groups from ten in the morning until four in the afternoon. Meanwhile, they also killed any elderly or disabled people they found in their homes who could not flee. Among them was 80-year-old Dim. Mathioudakis, who was killed in his bed, and Emm. Grisbolakis, paralyzed since birth. The 20-year-old Matheos Sygellakis was also killed by a bayonet inside his house. Of those to be executed, six survived, but three later died from their injuries."

According to the report, 117 people were killed in Amiras alone, with many families mourning the loss of up to ten members. Similar horrors unfolded in the other villages targeted by German reprisals.

See: Nikos Kazantzakis, Ioannis Kalitsounakis and Ioannis Kakridis, *Έκθεσις της Κεντρικής Επιτροπής Διαπιστώσεως Ωμοτήτων εν Κρήτη [Report of the Central Committee for the Determination of Atrocities in Crete], (*Heraklion: Municipality of Heraklion, 1983), 45.

38 In his Memoirs, Bandouvas expressed the opinion that his men killed over 100 of their

enemies:

"During the Battle of Viannos, which lasted approximately five days, according to our information, 453 [men] were killed, but that was not true. They were killed fewer.

They were killed approximately 100 men, maybe more, when the groups [of the guerrillas] entered Viannos province to confront the Germans.

During the Battle of Viannos itself on 12 September, they were killed, one of us, and two were injured. The others were killed in different places inside Viannos and the villages, inside the Germans' area" (Sanoudakis, *Op. Cit.*, 333). However, those claims, compared to the German reports, were false.

39 Kazantzakis, Kalitsounakis and Kakridis, *Op. Cit.,* 53-54.

40 Sanoudakis, *Op. Cit.*, 334.

41 Beevor, *Op. Cit.,* p. 153.

42 Hellenic Army History Directorate, Announcement of German Commander of Crete regarding Bandouvas, 17-11-1943.

43 *Ibid,* p. 153.

44 Hellenic Army History Directorate, Emmanouil Bandouvas' report about the Cretan National Resistance, 20-8-1945.

45 Koukounas, *Op. Cit.,* pp. 130-131.

Between Two Worlds: Mattis, Conviction, and Politics in the Fallujah Ceasefire

Mason Krebsbach

American Military University

ABSTRACT

His reputation as a warrior-scholar with a transformational leadership style and high-risk tolerance. His fierce determination earned him the moniker "Mad Dog," a name he was not entirely fond of. Analysis of the decision-making processes tends to focus on actions proposed by various individuals; however, this article provides discourse on the heavy burden of command. Despite his abilities and reputation, General James Mattis found himself negotiating a ceasefire he vehemently opposed in Fallujah, Iraq, in 2004. By examining Mattis's actions, one can understand how General James "Mad Dog" Mattis, the warrior-scholar, made peace by deciding against his very nature.

Keywords: Mattis, Marine Corps, warrior-scholar, Fallujah, Iraq, leadership, determination, command, ceasefire, decision-making

Entre dos mundos: Mattis, la convicción y la política en el alto el fuego de Faluya

RESUMEN

Su reputación como guerrero-erudito con un estilo de liderazgo transformador y una alta tolerancia al riesgo. Su férrea determinación le valió el apodo de "Mad Dog", un nombre que no le gustaba del todo. El análisis de los procesos de toma de decisiones suele centrarse en las acciones propuestas por diversos individuos; sin embargo, este artículo ofrece un discurso sobre la pesada carga del mando. A pesar de sus habilidades y reputación, el general James Mattis se vio obligado a negociar un alto el fuego al que se opuso vehementemente en Faluya, Irak, en 2004. Al examinar las acciones de Mattis, se puede comprender cómo el general James "Mad Dog" Mattis, el guerrero-erudito, logró la paz al decidir en contra de su propia naturaleza.

Palabras clave: Mattis, Cuerpo de Marines, guerrero-erudito, Falu-

doi: 10.18278/mhc.2.2.5

ya, Irak, liderazgo, determinación, mando, alto el fuego, toma de decisiones

两个世界之间：费卢杰停火协定中的马蒂斯、信念与政治

摘要

他以"战士兼学者"著称，拥有变革型领导风格和高风险承受能力。他坚定的决心为他赢得了"疯狗"的绰号，而他本人并不太喜欢这个名字。对决策过程的分析往往侧重于不同个人提出的行动方案；然而，本文探讨了指挥的沉重负担。尽管詹姆斯·马蒂斯将军拥有出色的能力和声誉，但他在2004年于伊拉克费卢杰参与了一项他强烈反对的停火谈判。通过分析马蒂斯的行动，我们能理解这位"战士兼学者"的詹姆斯·"疯狗"·马蒂斯将军是如何通过违背自身本性作出决定来缔造和平的。

关键词：马蒂斯，海军陆战队，战士兼学者，费卢杰，伊拉克，领导力，决心，指挥，停火，决策

Introduction: Mattis: How the Warrior Monk Was Chosen to Face the Dilemmas of Modern Warfare

One would be hard-pressed to identify a current member of the Department of Defense unfamiliar with General James Mattis (U.S. Marine Corps, retired). From being described as a warrior-scholar to earning the nickname "Mad Dog" and comically appearing in depictions mimicking religious paintings, Mattis became somewhat of a mythical figure in the eyes of military members, specifically young Marines. Much of the military lore surrounding Mattis stems from his time commanding the 1st Marine Division in Iraq from 2002 to 2004. However, civilian attention on Mattis grew when President Trump signed Public Law 115-2, to eliminate the prohibition of the appointment of an individual to serve as Secretary within 7 years of retirement.[1]

The reactions were split. Many military members felt Mattis was an extraordinary pick, and his hesitation in negotiating a ceasefire in Fallujah, Iraq, demonstrated an understanding of what needed to be done to meet strategic objectives. Others felt that the ceasefire was enacted far too late, alleging high numbers of civilian casualties under Mattis's command.[2] Regardless of one's perceptions of Mattis or the timing of the ceasefire in Fallujah, all individuals interested in the event should consider the application of both social learning theory and cognitive psychology. While studying the cognitive processes of Mattis would undoubtedly offer insight into his perceptions, problem-solving, use language, and decision-making, his reputation as a warrior monk or warrior scholar suggests his processes may have been influenced by observational learning or modeling, as is the case with social learning theory.

Both disciplines assist in explaining why Mattis negotiated a ceasefire no sooner and no later than April of 2004. However, before delving into why General James Mattis rationalized the negotiation of a ceasefire, it must be understood that the term "rational" is used to describe behavior that is deemed appropriate to specified goals within the context of a given situation.[3]

Why Mattis?

Analysis of the decision-making processes tends to focus on decisions as imagined, proposed, argued, and conducted by various individuals. The Mattis-Fallujah scenario deviates from this model, as Mattis opposed a ceasefire. It was not his "brainchild," an idea he supported, or an action he advocated for. He remains quite vocal about his opposition to the Fallujah ceasefire he negotiated, yet he complied with his directives. An examination of Mattis's begrudging compliance stands out in academic literature because it offers a case of actions rather than words about strategic implications.

Fallujah: The Background

To better understand Mattis's hesitation to negotiate a ceasefire, one must first understand the strategic value of Fallujah, Iraq. Fallujah rests along the Euphrates River in eastern Al Anbar Province, approximately 37 miles west of Baghdad, and in 2004, the population, primarily Sunni Muslim, was estimated at 300,000 inhabitants.[4] Due to its proximity to Baghdad and significant population density, the city had become a major focal point of U.S. military operations when the U.S. Army's 82nd Airborne Division arrived the year prior.[5] Although the U.S. military had encountered harsh resistance since establishing a presence in 2003, the city gained significant international attention when four American private security contractors were ambushed and killed by insurgents while they were driving through the city on March 31, 2004.[6]

The incident sparked strong emotional reactions from the U.S. military leaders, including then-Major General James Mattis, Commander of the 1st Marine Division; however, in speaking with Colonel Joseph F. Dunford, Mattis was advised that sending in troops to recover the contractors' bodies could result in significant civilian casualties.[7] Dunford recommended that the Marines avoid military action to allow the situation to calm down, and Mattis agreed, stating that rushing in made "no sense."[8] Despite the reservations of Mattis and Dunford, the U.S. government decided that the appropriate reaction was a show of force. Under the guidance of Secretary of Defense Donald H. Rumsfeld, President George W. Bush ordered the launch of Operation Vigilant Resolve to regain control of Fallujah.[9]

Operation Vigilant Resolve was characterized by levels of intense urban combat unseen since the 1968 Battle of Hue City, a pivotal event of the Tet Offensive in which North Vietnamese forces trapped U.S. Marines in a grueling house-to-house fight through the use of heavy weaponry and close-quar-

ters combat techniques.[10] As was the case in 1968 Vietnam, 2004 Iraq forced U.S. Marines to reclaim territory house by house and block by block. The operation was perceived as "heavy-handed" by members of the interim Iraqi government and the international community and was quickly met with severe criticism and political pressure.[11] The backlash against the operation eventually led to a ceasefire, negotiated by General Mattis, which would have significant implications for the future conflict in Fallujah. According to various

WASHINGTON (Jan. 25, 2016) Official portrait of Secretary of Defense James N. Mattis. (U.S. Army photo by Monica King/Released), https://picryl.com/me dia/170125-a-ss368-005-32208929170-210cc1

accounts, including General Mattis's testimony, he opposed the ceasefire that the Iraqi government and the U.S. military leadership enacted. General Mattis stated on multiple occasions that he believed the ceasefire was premature and that it allowed the insurgents to regroup and recover. He also said that he was concerned that the ceasefire would undermine the momentum of the operation and allow the enemy to escape and reorganize.

Mattis Asking Himself, "What-if?" – The Use of Counterfactuals

Decisions are seldom made in a vacuum or under ideal circumstances. Action is often forced during tragedy, crisis, change, or high-stakes scenarios. Leaders, decision-makers, and policy advisers attempt to manage their emotional responses and focus on problem-solving under pressure using a valuable practice known as "counterfactual thinking."[12] Counterfactual thinking—asking "what if" or "what might have been"—involves considering alternative scenarios or outcomes. This process allows leaders to imagine different courses of action and their potential consequences.[13]

Counterfactuals differ from traditional analysis, which relies on vetted data, trends, and polished intelligence products. Instead, counterfactuals focus on what could happen or could have happened—e.g., worst-case scenarios. This technique is especially valuable when dealing with low-probability but high-impact events, as it encourages individuals to question or abandon assumptions, develop a shared understanding of risk, and reduce biases.[14]

General James Mattis almost certainly used counterfactuals. While scholars lack access to the classified briefings or the reports reviewed by Mattis, his leadership style, public statements, and historic events offer clues to counterfactuals' impact on his decision-making. Marine doctrine itself encourages counterfactual thinking. The 1997 U.S. Marine Corps document *MCDP 1*, titled *Warfighting*, advocates considering both the possible and probable when planning operations.[15] Similarly, the 1990 manual, *FMFM-1-1, Campaigning*, emphasizes the need for flexibility and the inevitability of uncertainty.[16] Mattis would have been intimately familiar with these documents, their successors, and the principles they outline.

Additionally, two years before the first siege of Fallujah—known as Operation Vigilant Resolve—the U.S. Department of Defense conducted a large joint counterfactual training exercise called Millennium Challenge 2002 (MC02). This multimillion-dollar exercise was set in a fictional country, with the combat scenario based on enemy capabilities projected for the then-not-so-distant future of 2007.[17] Despite its ambitious goals, MC02 was critically flawed. Planners had given the red (enemy) team artificially limited capabilities and scripted motives. However, the red team defied expectations and sank the "friendly" team's entire naval carrier group in a surprise move, ending

U.S. Marine Corps Sgt. Chambers briefs other Marines on the day's schedule in Fallujah, Iraq, on Nov. 11, 2004. The Marines, assigned to Regimental Combat Team Seven, 1st Battalion, 3rd Charlie Company, are preparing to clear the houses surrounding their current position inside the city of Fallujah. Defense.gov News Photo 041111-M-8096K-002 - PICRYL - Public Domain Media Search Engine Public Domain Search

the exercise in 10 minutes.[18] Although MC02 was a large, expensive failure, it highlighted the importance of flexibility, contingencies, and the limitations of rigid plans.

Mattis was not a planner for MC02, but he and other leaders likely studied these lessons and understood the importance of asking "what if" and preparing for the unexpected. For Mattis and other individuals like him, counterfactual thinking wasn't theoretical—it had practical applications. It is highly probable that, during briefings or when reviewing relevant reports, Mattis asked himself and those around

him "what if" to ensure his forces were prepared for the complexities of Fallujah. The same approach can be assessed when he was tasked with negotiating a ceasefire in Fallujah.

What Can Be Won and Lost? Mattis and Prospect Theory

As mentioned above, the theory of counterfactuals often addresses low probability but high-impact events. These events are regularly analyzed in terms of potential gains and losses, requiring decision-makers to assess acceptable levels of risk. One theory commonly used to study risk acceptance or aversion is "borrowed" from behavioral economics: Prospect Theory. This theory examines how individuals make choices when faced with uncertainty or risk.

Prospect Theory deviates from rational decision-making models that rely on evaluating objective data. Instead, it focuses on how individuals perceive potential gains and losses relative to their current situation or "reference point."[19] Key elements of Prospect Theory include:

- Reference Dependence
- Loss Aversion
- Diminishing Sensitivity
- Probability Weighting.[20]

These elements explain why leaders may become hyper-focused on low-probability threats rather than predictable events or experience "paralysis by analysis" when faced with potential losses. The case of General Mattis and Fallujah offers a compelling example of Prospect Theory in decision-making under uncertainty. After the deaths of four private security contractors on March 31, 2004, General Mattis faced immense pressure to respond appropriately. However, the term "appropriate" was subjective at the time. Some considered military action the most suitable response, while others advocated for economic measures to undermine insurgent support among civilians.

Notably, in 2004, while most of Fallujah's 250,000–300,000 residents were not insurgents, they weren't necessarily receptive to Coalition forces.[21]

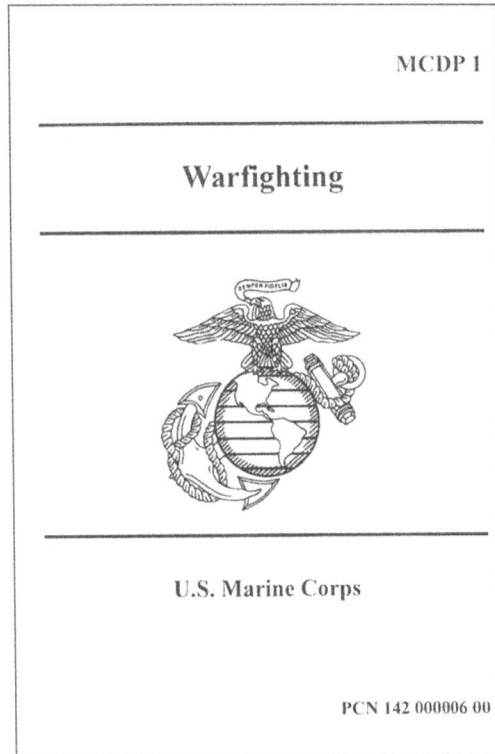

MCDP 1

Warfighting

U.S. Marine Corps

PCN 142 000006 00

Mattis faced a dilemma: overreaction that risked alienating what little civilian support existed, while inaction could allow insurgents to regroup. Both scenarios threatened the Coalition's ability to maintain control of Fallujah. Despite Mattis using the loss of Fallujah as his reference point, he negotiated a ceasefire and turned control of the city over to the Iraqi military. He later described this decision as one of the hardest he ever made.[22]

Swimming Against the Current: Mattis and Bureaucracy

Addressing collaboration and communication between the Department of Defense and the Executive Branch without discussing the bureaucratic environment is difficult at best. Many government initiatives and mandates argue the need to be unified. However, governments often operate as collections of individuals and departments with differing goals and priorities. This means that governments, including the American government, do not always function as a single, unified, rational actor. Instead, they operate as competitive arenas composed of multiple stakeholders with non-negotiable values; consequently, simplicity and clarity often fall by the wayside.

For General James Mattis, the complexities and frustrations of such an environment were a constant reality during his time in Iraq. Fallujah, in particular, was a web of U.S. and coalition forces, insurgents, Iraqi soldiers, Iraqi police, and non-combatants. Each group had its own agenda, ideology, and acceptable level of risk.[23] While Mattis's subordinates were as prepared as possible—studying 1,000 pages of material on insurgencies[24]—they still encountered significant bureaucratic obstacles, such as the Iraqi Governing Council's threat to resign.[25]

When tasked with negotiating a ceasefire, Mattis expressed dissatisfaction with the process but understood the limits of his authority within the larger government bureaucracy. Years later, he sought to prepare junior Marines for similar challenges, urging them to prioritize mental preparation for navigating bureaucratic structures. He advised, "Go through the mental gyrations now."[26] In 2018, reflecting on larger bureaucratic institutions such as NATO, Mattis remarked, "Every one of them has its interests, its perspective, but at the end of the day, NATO was stronger than ever."[27] Although Mattis often voiced frustrations with bureaucratic institutions, he also emphasized balancing internal rivalries with the pursuit of shared goals.

When Leaders Are Too Involved: Mattis and Leadership

The majority of academic research on leadership focuses on powerful, centralized figures such as autocrats or monarchs;[28] however, modern scholarship is evolving to include democratic leaders or those with authorities bestowed upon them as part of a larger system. James Mattis would fall into the latter category, as he operated within the military chain of command, and the structures of the Department of Defense granted him authority. No matter the source of authority, leaders find their influences in a cultural context.[29] From this similarity, leaders fall under one of two categories of what Julian B. Rotter refers to as the "Locus of Control." Those with an Internal Locus of Control perceive a direct connection between their behavior and the rewards or punishments they receive. Leaders with an External Locus of Control believe there is very little connection between their behavior and the outcomes they experience. Both forms of Locus, per Rotter, are deeply influenced by experiences, such as social and cultural influences, organizational measurement and assessments, and individual interactions.[30] These individual factors merge to define a leader's ability to clarify principles, assess relationships, and control behavior.[31]

Camp Pendleton, Calif. (Jul. 30, 2002) -- A Light Armored Command and Control Vehicle is unloaded from the experimental High-Speed Vessel "Joint Venture" (HSV-X1) to an expeditionary causeway in the Del Mar Boat Basin aboard Camp Pendleton, during an experimental evaluation of the exceptional maneuverability of this ship. Joint Venture is participating in the Navy's "Fleet Battle Experiment Juliet." Juliet is a part of Joint Forces Command's "Millennium Challenge 2002" (MC-02). MC-02 is the nation's premier joint integrating event, bringing together both live field exercises and computer simulations throughout the Department of Defense. U.S. Navy photo by Photographer's Mate 2nd Class Aaron Ansarov. (RELEASED) https://picryl.com/media/us-navy-020730-n-4309a-007-light-armored-vehicles-unload-from-joint-venture-41c62f

General Mattis was described by many as a transformational leader, meaning he made conscious attempts to inspire and motivate others to achieve shared objectives while they also achieved personal growth. His efforts could also be seen in what the National University called the "Four 'I's" of transformational leadership.[32] The first I, **Intellectual Stimulation**, was demonstrated when Mattis tasked his battalions to become familiar with Arab customs and language to foster cultural understanding.[33] **Individual Consideration**, the second I, was evident when Mattis explained leaders' responsibility to their teams. At the U.S. Naval Academy, he stated, "A tragedy is when one of your beloved young sailors or Marines ... does something, and now you have to court-martial him. That is the last thing you ever want to do because you failed to talk your people through it."[34]

Mattis is probably best known for his striking quotes that emphasized and glorified **Inspirational Motivation**, the third I. Mattis has shared several famous anecdotes like, "Be polite, be professional, but have a plan to kill everybody you meet" and "Your moral crisis will come to you ... when you are dead-tired."[35] Finally, despite his fame and reputation, General Mattis modeled humility in his demonstration and embodiment of the final I, **Idealized Influence**. In 2004, he told reporters, "I get a lot of credit these days for things I never did."[36] Surprisingly, the desirable leadership style of Mattis, which focuses on individualism, can also present several obstacles in strategic environments. National University argues that transformational leadership complicates decision-making, increases the need for communication, disrupts organizations, and risks leaders losing control of their teams.[37] In the case of Mattis and Fallujah, his leadership style placed his efforts on internal factors and personal control, while those around him prioritized external factors like Iraqi militia actions or civilian dynamics. This stark contrast between Mattis and his fellow leaders sheds light on Mattis's objection to negotiating a ceasefire.

Conclusion

The forced negotiation of a ceasefire in Fallujah, Iraq, provides significant insight into how decision-makers and leaders use cognitive processes and heuristics to rationalize actions. Mattis attempted to control the external environment through the utilization of the "four 'I's" of transformational leadership: intellectual stimulation, individual consideration, inspirational motivation, and idealized influence.

Unfortunately, Mattis's leadership style and personal ambitions were not enough to manage the complexity of Fallujah, the international community, or the American bureaucratic system. This is not to say that Mattis was naïve or overestimated his capabilities. His ambitions and ideals were shaped by his use of counterfactual thinking, considering alternative outcomes and predictions in "what-if" scenarios.

His warrior-scholar methodology—a combination of the "four 'I's" and counterfactual thinking applied to real-world challenges—helped establish his reference points within Iraq. These reference points contributed to a higher level of risk acceptance than many of his fellow Marines. Ultimately, however, Mattis's cognitive processes and relative authority within a bureaucratic system were insufficient to convince decision-makers to carry out further military action in Fallujah. Nonetheless, he actively participated in the negotiations, demonstrating flexibility and adaptability.

About the Author

Mason Krebsbach holds multiple degrees, including an AAS degree in Aircraft Maintenance Technology and Intelligence Studies from the Community College of the Air Force (2015), a BS in Terrorism and Counterterrorism Studies from Henley-Putnam University (2017), and an MA in Military Studies from American Military University (2020). He has authored numerous publications on military history and presented his research on Indigenous-Federal Intelligence collaboration at the Dupont Security Summit (2024).

Endnotes

1   U.S. Department of Defense, Millennium Challenge 2002 Experiment Report (Washington, D.C.: Joint Staff, 2002), https://www.esd.whs.mil/Portals/54/Documents/FOID/Reading%20 Room/Joint_Staff/12-F-0344-Millennium-Challenge-2002-Experiment-Report.pdf.

2   Aaron Glantz, "Did Defense Secretary Nominee James Mattis Commit War Crimes in Iraq?" *Reveal News*, January 11, 2017, https://revealnews.org/article/did-defense-secretary-nominee-james-mattis-commit-war-crimes-in-iraq/.

3   Herbert A. Simon, "Human Nature in Politics: The Dialogue of Psychology with Political Science," *The American Political Science* Review 79, no. 2 (1985): 294, https://doi.org/10.2307/1956650.

4   Paul Bremer III, *My Year in Iraq: The Struggle to Build a Future of Hope* (New York: Simon & Schuster, 2006), 313.

5   Vincent Foulk, *The Battle for Fallujah: Occupation, Resistance and Stalemate in the War in Iraq* (Jefferson: McFarland & Company, 2007), 6.

6   Gerald De Lira Jr., "The Anger of a Great Nation: Operation Vigilant Resolve," Master of Military Studies thesis, Marine Corps University, 2005, ii, https://apps.dtic.mil/sti/tr/pdf/ADA509044.pdf.

7   Bing West, *No True Glory: A Frontline Account of the Battle for Fallujah* (New York: Bantam Dell, 2005), 4.

8   Ibid., 4.

9   Gerald De Lira Jr., "The Anger of a Great Nation: Operation Vigilant Resolve," Master of Military Studies thesis, Marine Corps University, 2005, ii, https://apps.dtic.mil/sti/tr/pdf/ADA509044.pdf.

10 Andrew J. Lawler, "The Battle for Hué City," *Proceedings* 125, no. 7 (July 1999), https://www.usni.org/magazines/proceedings/1999/july/battle-hue-city.

11 Ibid., ii.

12 Mamta Tripathi and Bharatendu Nath Srivastava, "When and How Does Counterfactual

Thinking Prevent Catastrophes and Foster Group Decision Accuracy?" *International Journal of Conflict Management* 27, no. 2 (2016): 250, https://doi.org/10.1108/IJCMA-02-20150008.

13 K. Epstude and N.J. Roese, "The Functional Theory of Counterfactual Thinking," *Personality and Social Psychology Review* 12, no. 2 (2008): 168-92, https://doi.org/10.1177/1088868308318666.

14 Nate Huber, "What If Analysis: Exploring Alternative Futures," War Room, January 5, 2023, https://warroom.armywarcollege.edu/articles/what-if/#:~:text=%E2%80%9CWhat%20If%20 analysis%E2%80%9D%20is%20a,get%20to%20that%20future%20point; and F.C. Brodbeck, R. Kerschreiter, A. Mojzisch, D. Frey, and S. Schulz-Hardt, "The Dissemination of Critical, Unshared Information in Decision-Making Groups: The Effects of Prediscussion Dissent," *European Journal of Social Psychology* 32, no. 1 (2002): 35-56, https://doi.org/10.1002/ejsp.74.

15 U.S. Marine Corps, *MCDP 1: Warfighting* (Washington, D.C.: Department of the Navy, 1997), https://www.marines.mil/portals/1/publications/mcdp%201%20warfighting.pdf.

16 U.S. Marine Corps, FMFM 1-1: Campaigning (Washington, D.C.: Department of the Navy, 1990), https://www.globalsecurity.org/military/library/policy/usmc/fmfm/1-1/fmfm1-1.pdf.

17 Micah Zenko, "Millennium Challenge: The Real Story of a Corrupted Military Exercise and Its Legacy," *War on the Rocks*, November 5, 2015, https://warontherocks.com/2015/11/millenni um-challenge-the-real-story-of-a-corrupted-military-exercise-and-its-legacy/.

18 Ibid.

19 Nicholas C. Barberis, "Thirty Years of Prospect Theory in Economics: A Review and Assessment," *Journal of Economic Perspectives* 27, no. 1 (2013): 173–96; and Jonathan Mercer, "Prospect Theory and Political Science," *Annual Review of Political Science* 8, no. 1 (2005): 1–21, https://doi.org/10.1146/annurev.polisci.8.082103.104911.

20 Ibid., 173–96.

21 United States Marine Corps University, "Fallujah: A Study in Counterinsurgency" (United States Marine Corps University, April 2009), accessed December 9, 2024, https://www.usmcu. edu/Portals/218/FALLUJAH.pdf.

22 Glantz, 2017.

23 George W. Bush Presidential Library and Museum, "The Iraq War," George W. Bush Presidential Library, accessed December 9, 2024, https://www.georgewbushlibrary.gov/research/ topic-guides/the-iraq-war.

24 Thomas E. Ricks, "Fiasco," Armed Forces Journal, August 1, 2006, http://armedforcesjournal. com/fiasco/

25 John Spencer and Jayson Geroux, "Urban Warfare Case Study #6: First Battle of Fallujah," *Modern War Institute at West Point*, October 27, 2020, https://mwi.westpoint.edu/urban-warfare-case-study-6-first-battle-of-fallujah/.

26 United States Naval Academy. Lecture by Lieutenant General James N. Mattis. February 23, 2006 https://www.usna.edu/Ethics/_files/documents/MattisPg1-28_Final.pdf.

27 James Mattis, "Secretary Mattis Remarks on the National Defense Strategy in Conversation with," U.S. Department of Defense, October 30, 2018, accessed December 9, 2024, https://www.defense.gov/News/Transcripts/Transcript/Article/1678512/secretary-mattis-remarks-on-the-national-defense-strategy-in-conversation-with/.

28 Margaret G. Hermann, Thomas Preston, Baghat Korany, and Timothy M. Shaw, "Who Leads Matters: The Effects of Powerful Individuals," *International Studies Review* 3, no. 2 (2001): 85, https://doi.org/10.1111/1521-9488.00235.

29 Ibid., 83; John D. Stoessinger, Crusaders and Pragmatists: Movers of Modern American Foreign Policy (New York: W.W. Norton, 1979); and Peter Suedfeld, "Cognitive Misers and Their Critics," *Political Psychology* 13 (1992): 435–53.

30 W. L. Davis and E. J. Phares, "Internal-External Control as a Determinant of Information-Seeking in a Social Influence Situation," *Journal of Personality* 35 (1967): 547–61; and J. B. Rotter, "Generalized Expectancies for Internal Versus External Control of Reinforcement," *Psychological Monographs* 80 (1966): 1–28.

31 Judith Goldstein and Robert Keohane, "Ideas and Foreign Policy: An Analytical Framework," in *Ideas and Foreign Policy: Beliefs, Institutions, and Political Change*, ed. Judith Goldstein and Robert Keohane (Ithaca: Cornell University Press, 1993), 5.

32 "What Is Transformational Leadership?" National University, https://www.nu.edu/blog/what-is-transformational-leadership/.

33 Ricks, 2006.

34 United States Naval Academy. Lecture by Lieutenant General James N. Mattis. February 23, 2006 https://www.usna.edu/Ethics/_files/documents/MattisPg1-28_Final.pdf.

35 Madeleine Conway, "James Mattis Quotes," Politico, December 1, 2016, accessed December 9, 2024, https://www.politico.com/blogs/donald-trump-administration/2016/12/james-mattis-quotes-232097; and James Mattis, "Secretary Mattis Remarks on the National Defense Strategy in Conversation with," U.S. Department of Defense, October 30, 2018, accessed December 9, 2024, https://www.defense.gov/News/Transcripts/Transcript/Article/1678512/secretary-mattis-remarks-on-the-national-defense-strategy-in-conversation-with/.

36 The Week Staff, "Who Is James 'Mad Dog' Mattis, Donald Trump's Choice for Defence?" The Week, December 6, 2016, https://theweek.com/us-election-2016/79415/who-is-james-mad-dog-mattis-donald-trumps-choice-for-defence.

37 "What Is Transformational Leadership?" National University, accessed [Date Accessed], https://www.nu.edu/blog/what-is-transformational-leadership/.

Bibliography

Ambassador 1. Paul Bremer III, *My Year in Iraq: The Struggle to Build a Future of Hope* (New York: Simon & Schuster, 2006), 313.

Barberis, Nicholas C. 2013. "Thirty Years of Prospect Theory in Economics: A Review and Assessment." *Journal of Economic Perspectives* 27 (1): 173–96.

Brodbeck, F.C., Kerschreiter, R., Mojzisch, A., Frey, D. and Schulz-Hardt, S. 2002. "The dissemination of critical, unshared information in decision-making groups: the effects of prediscussion dissent," *European Journal of Social Psychology*, Vol. 32 No. 1, pp. 35–56. doi: 10.1002/ejsp.74

Conway, Madeleine. "James Mattis Quotes." *Politico*, December 1, 2016. Accessed December 9, 2024, https://www.politico.com/blogs/donald-trump-administration/2016/12/james-mattis-quotes-232097.

Davis, W. L., & Phares, E. J. 1967. "Internal-external control as a determinant of information-seeking in a social influence situation." *Journal of Personality*, 35, 547–561.

De Lira Jr., Gerald, Major, U.S.M.C. "The Anger of a Great Nation: Operation Vigilant Resolve." Master of Military Studies thesis, Marine Corps University, 2005. https://apps.dtic.mil/sti/tr/pdf/ADA509044.pdf.

Epstude, K. and Roese, N. J. 2008. "The functional theory of counterfactual thinking." *Personality and Social Psychology Review*, Vol. 12 No. 2, pp. 168–192. doi: 10.1177/1088868

Foulk, Vincent, *The Battle for Fallujah: Occupation, Resistance and Stalemate in the War in Iraq* (Jefferson, McFarland & Company, 2007), 6.

Galinsky, A. D. and Kray, L. J. 2004. "From thinking about what might have been to sharing what we know: the effects of counterfactual mind-sets on information sharing in groups." *Journal of Experimental Social Psychology*, Vol. 40 No. 5, pp. 606–618. doi: 10.1016/j.jesp.2003.11.005.

George W. Bush Presidential Library and Museum. "The Iraq War." *George W. Bush Presidential Library*. Accessed December 9, 2024. https://www.georgewbush library.gov/research/topic-guides/the-iraq-war

Glantz, Aaron. "Did Defense Secretary Nominee James Mattis Commit War Crimes in Iraq?" Reveal News, January 11, 2017. https://revealnews.org/article/

did-defense-secretary-nominee-james-mattis-commit-war-crimes-in-iraq/.

Goldstein, Judith, and Robert Keohane. 1993. "Ideas and Foreign Policy: An An-alytical Framework." In *Ideas and Foreign Policy: Beliefs, Institutions, and Political*

Change, edited by Judith Goldstein and Robert Keohane. Ithaca: Cornell University Press. Hermann, Margaret G., Thomas Preston, Baghat Korany, and Timothy M. Shaw. 2001. "Who Leads Matters: The Effects of Powerful Individuals." *International Studies Review* 3 (2): 83. doi:10.1111/1521-9488.00235

Huber, Nate. "What If Analysis: Exploring Alternative Futures." *War Room*, January 5, 2023, https://warroom.armywarcollege.edu/articles/what-if/#:~:text=%E 2%80%9CWhat%20If%20analysis%E2%80%9D%20is%20a,get%20to%20 that%20future%20point.

Lawler, Andrew J. "The Battle for Hué City." *Proceedings* 125, no. 7 (July 1999), https://www.usni.org/magazines/proceedings/1999/july/battle-hue-city.

Mattis, James. "Secretary Mattis Remarks on the National Defense Strategy in Conversation with." U.S. Department of Defense, October 30, 2018. Accessed December 9, 2024, https://www.defense.gov/News/Transcripts/Transcript/Arti cle/1678512/secretary-mattis-remarks-on-the-national-defense-strategy-in-con versation-with/.

Mercer, Jonathan. 2005. "Prospect Theory and Political Science." *Annual Review of Political Science* 8 (1): 1–21. doi:10.1146/annurev.polisci.8.082103.104911.

Ricks, Thomas E. "Fiasco." *Armed Forces Journal*, August 1, 2006. http://armed-forcesjournal.com/fiasco/.

Rotter, J. B. 1966. "Generalized expectancies for internal versus external control of reinforcement." *Psychological Monographs*, 80, 1–28.

Simon, Herbert A. "Human Nature in Politics: The Dialogue of Psychology with Political Science." *The American Political Science Review* 79, no. 2 (1985): 293–304. https://doi.org/10.2307/1956650.

Spencer, John and Jayson Geroux. "Urban Warfare Case Study #6: First Battle of Fallujah." *Modern War Institute at West Point*, October 27, 2020, https://mwi.west point.edu/urban-warfare-case-study-6-first-battle-of-fallujah/

Stoessinger, John D. 1979. *Crusaders and Pragmatists: Movers of Modern American Foreign Policy*. New York: W. W. Norton.

Suedfeld, Peter. 1992. "Cognitive Misers and Their Critics." *Political Psychology* 13: 435–453.

Tripathi, Mamta and Bharatendu Nath Srivastava. 2016. "When and how does Counterfactual Thinking Prevent Catastrophes and Foster Group Decision Accuracy." *International Journal of Conflict Management* 27 (2): 249–274. doi:https://doi.org/10.1108/IJCMA-02-20150008. http://ezproxy.apus.edu/login?qurl=https%3A%2F%2Fwww.proquest.com%2Fscholarly-journals%2Fwhen-how-does-counterfactual-thinking-prevent%2Fdocview%2F1881794387%2Fse-2%3Faccountid%3D8289

United States Department of Defense. "James N. Mattis." History.Defense.gov. Accessed December 10, 2024. https://history.defense.gov/Multimedia/Biographies/Article-View/Article/1059855/james-n-mattis/

United States Marine Corps University. "Fallujah: A Study in Counterinsurgency." United States Marine Corps University, April 2009. Accessed December 9, 2024, https://www.usmcu.edu/Portals/218/FALLUJAH.pdf.

United States Naval Academy. Lecture by Lieutenant General James N. Mattis. February 23, 2006, https://www.usna.edu/Ethics/_files/documents/MattisPg1-28_Final.pdf.

U.S. Department of Defense, *Millennium Challenge 2002 Experiment Report* (Washington, D.C.: Joint Staff, 2002), https://www.esd.whs.mil/Portals/54/Documents/FOID/Reading%20Room/Joint_Staff/12-F-0344-Millennium-Challenge-2002-Experiment-Report.pdf.

U.S. Marine Corps. FMFM 1-1: Campaigning. Washington, D.C.: Department of the Navy, 1990. https://www.globalsecurity.org/military/library/policy/usmc/fmfm/1-1/fmfm1-1.pdf.

U.S. Marine Corps. MCDP 1: Warfighting. Washington, D.C.: Department of the Navy, 1997. https://www.marines.mil/portals/1/publications/mcdp%201%20warfighting.pdf.

West, Bing. *No True Glory: A Frontline Account of the Battle for Fallujah* (New York: Bantam Dell, 2005), 4.

Zenko, Micah. "Millennium Challenge: The Real Story of a Corrupted Military Exercise and Its Legacy." *War on the Rocks*, published on November 5, 2015. https://warontherocks.com/2015/11/millennium-challenge-the-real-story-of-a-corrupted-military-exercise-and-its-legacy/.

Book Review: Andrew Eric Wright Sr.'s *Death Before Dismount: U.S. Army Tanks in Iraq*

Dr. Robert Young

Professor
Department of History and Military History
American Military University

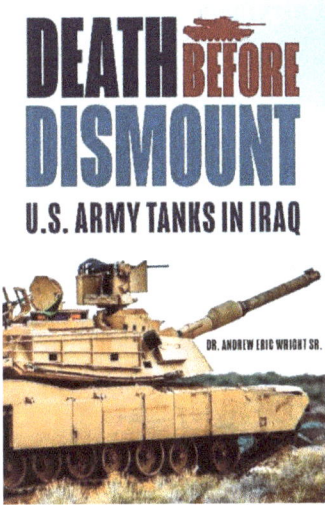

Wright Sr., Andrew Eric. *Death Before Dismount: U.S. Army Tanks in Iraq.* Havertown, PA.: Casemate, 2025. ISBN 978-1636244754. Pp. 256. Hardcover $31.71. Electronic version available.

Andrew Eric Wright Sr.'s *Death Before Dismount: U.S. Army Tanks in Iraq* offers an analysis of U.S. armor during Operatio*n Iraqi Freedom*, the war in Iraq that began with the American invasion during the spring of 2003. The author served in Iraq (Ramadi, Baqubah, Sadr City) on various deployments between 2006 and 2008, an experience evident throughout this work, making it a primary source. The author argues that Army tanks were essential during the war in Iraq and analyzes the role of armor from the war's initial invasion to the vicious street fighting that took place once the insurgency in Iraq began in the summer of 2003.

The majority of *Death Before Dismount* is both informative and revealing. Wright dedicates a chapter to the Battle of Fallujah, a battle for which the Marine Corps is justifiably proud. The author highlights the vital role played by the Army's M1A2 Abrams in that victory, a fact that few seem to recognize. To the casual observer or reader through the press, in discussions, and in the many books published on the Battle of Fallujah, the Marines are <u>spoken</u> of as if they were the only ones fighting in the city. *Death Before Dismount* corrects that fallacy.

Wright presents a glowing appreciation of Iraqi military capabilities

doi: 10.18278/mhc.2.2.6

during the initial invasion. As the invasion moved towards Baghdad, the fighting was fierce. Tanks spearheaded the invasion, engaging older Soviet-model Iraqi tanks, such as the T-62 and T-72. Individual commanders, from battalion to platoon level, are the focus of the story, and the roles they played in various battles are highlighted. The author introduces the reader to the Captains (Company Commanders), Lieutenants (Executive Officers and Platoon Leaders), and individual tank commanders (Sergeants). These were not large-scale battles but rather close-quarter fights, where a single tank or, at most, a platoon supported an operation. Wright describes individual exploits and lets the reader know the men who performed those exploits.

The reader will learn that tank crews were being used as foot soldiers due to a shortage of infantry, particularly after 2006. The author points out that in the environment of the Iraqi War, following the onset of the insurgency, armor officers and crewmen had to be equally adept at both tank operations and cavalry tactics. I knew officers needed both capabilities. They are not trained for that, but were forced to learn in the theater. Members of tank crews often dismounted and were involved in patrols and clearing of buildings.

The author highlights what many are aware of from the extensive news coverage during this war. Despite the billions of dollars poured into Iraq by the U.S. government, the military forces were poorly trained and motivated, and there was little the American forces

could do about the enduring hatred between the Sunni and Shia sects. Here, the soldiers come through. As someone who witnessed and operated in this environment, he presents the war he observed with clarity. The author intended this book to describe the role of armor in the war, but unintentionally, he also illustrates other facets, such as tankers serving as infantrymen.

Veterans of this war and the war in Afghanistan speak frequently of Rules of Engagement (ROE). This was not World War II, where codified ROE did not exist. However, some standards were expected to be followed. In Iraq, American tanks roamed the towns and cities of Iraq, firing upon an enemy interspersed with the civilian population. There were many times they could not return fire because the ROE required positive identification of the enemy. The author, along with others who fought there, was frustrated with the limitations; yet, he acknowledges their necessity in the environment of Iraq.

Wright also takes a subtle shot at the media for their less-than-honorable reporting. During 2008, U.S. forces were barred from Sadr City unless they received permission from Iraqi Prime Minister Nouri al-Maliki. In October 2007, U.S. Special Forces launched a mission in Sadr City to capture an insurgent leader. Eighty enemy fighters attacked the Special Forces Group, and in a heavy firefight within the city, an airstrike was requested. That airstrike killed over forty of the enemy, but also tragically, civilians. The fact that U.S. forces were attacked did not seem to matter, and U.S. news and media outlets led with stories that America was indiscriminately killing civilians. The frustration of those who fought there is evident.

Another level of frustration felt by armored officers and enlisted men alike was occurring around the time of the operation just described. Tanks were not used in that operation. A drive to phase out armor had begun, where tank crews were even being converted to Humvees to provide additional infantry. That quickly changed. Tanks could have provided direct fire support without the unfortunate collateral damage of an airstrike. As Wright points out: "The siege of Sadr city was proof that the war was far from settled and the tanks were always necessary for any major combat operation." (131) The absence of enemy armor after the war's first days did not negate the vitality of armor as an infantry support weapon.

There are some concerns in this work. The publisher must do a more thorough job of editing a submission. There are some basic writing errors, and particularly in the early portion of the book, it seems repetitive. These are problems that editorial diligence would eliminate. However, it is a factual error on the book's third page that struck me: "From the time General Patton instituted an armor training center for tankers after World War II, tankers have benefited from the style of soldiering that could only be found in armor units." (3) For a soldier and military historian such as Dr. Wright to make such an error is puzzling. Patton, one of the

pioneers of American armor, died right after World War II and never returned to the United States. He did play a role in creating such a school after World War I. I believe this is an error of the publisher, but a knowledgeable reader of military history would notice this immediately. The author also states that America did not have armor superiority in Vietnam, which is false. Further, he points out several times in his initial pages that U.S. Army armor units had the highest kill rates of any American armor units and were more effective at doing so. Compared to whom? Only the Marines also have armored formations, and they are limited in number. There is not much to measure that high kill rate and effectiveness against.

Approximately one-quarter of *Death Before Dismount* covers the training of both enlisted men and officers assigned to the armor branch. It explains the capabilities, both mechanically and in armament, of the M1A1 Main Battle Tank. This section does little to describe any training in tank-infantry cooperation or an urban environment. Other than during the first months of the Iraq invasion, American armor did not face Iraqi armor. The role of tanks changed, and training had to change with it, a point the author must make. The reader does not need a basic overview of how early basic training operates. There is also not much discussion of officer training and so on. this portion of the book is perhaps unnecessary.

Despite some early errors and a largely unnecessary and vague description of armored training methods, this is a very good description of the nuances of the war in Iraq and the role tanks played in it. The essence of this book is the description of those who fought there, on a personal level, and the tanks that took them into battle. Wright fought in this war, and his perspective lends humanity to *Death Before Dismount: U.S. Army Tanks in Iraq*. Published by Casemate, this book should be added to any historical library, particularly if a reader is interested in American military operations in Iraq.

About the Author

Robert Young earned a Ph.D. in Military History and Modern European Studies from the C.U.N.Y. Graduate Center in 2003 and a master's degree in American History from Brooklyn College in 1994. He is currently a History and Military History professor at American Military University. A veteran of the United States Army, he held various leadership positions in armored and cavalry units.

Book Review: *Bernhard Sindberg: The Schindler of Nanjing* by Peter Harmsen

Aisha Manus

Independent Historian

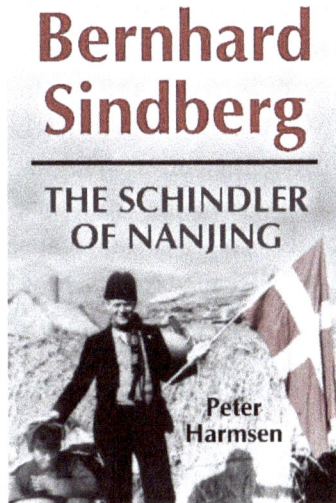

Harmsen, Peter. *Bernhard Sindberg: The Schindler of Nanjing*. Casemate Publishing, 2024. ISBN 9781636243313. Notes. Bibliography. Index. 67 b/w images. 226 pp.

Written to "contribute greater awareness in the West of a man who is already honored in the East" (vi), *Bernhard Sindberg: The Schindler of Nanjing* by Peter Harmsen enlightens readers to a forgotten piece of history but alas does so in a way I would like to forget. Initially, the writing drew me into the story, and I was eager to learn more. But that immersion just as quickly began to wear off as the book continued. By the end, I was glad it was over.

Beginning with a deep dive into the history of Bernhard Sindberg's family and his upbringing, the reader is given a deeper and greater understanding of the type of man he was and how he would come to be in Nanjing. From running away for the first time at age 2 to working on a ship at 16, Harmsen paints Sindberg as a man destined to travel the world. At 19, he joined the Foreign Legion before quickly deserting, a key fact repeated often for no real reason, it seems, other than to fill space. He then sailed to China, became a volunteer soldier there, and later the assistant of a famous war correspondent before finally ending up at a cement factory 26 miles outside of Nanjing as its keeper. This is where Harmsen attempts to argue that, because of Sindberg alone, many Chinese citizens were saved from the Japanese.

doi: 10.18278/mhc.2.2.7

Using the letters and journals of Sindberg, Harmsen paints in graphic detail the events that took place in China at the hands of the Japanese, while also interweaving the history of Nanjing and China throughout to give those who do not have prior knowledge of the events beforehand a solid background. Interesting facts throughout the book make it a continuous learning experience, and using Sindberg's own words strengthens the book. The book includes 67 black-and-white images, from photos of Sindberg to pictures of the places discussed, that create a portrait of Nanjing from 1937-1938. The maps, in particular, help give the reader a better understanding of the isolation of the cement factory he watches over during the occupation. To be blunt, without the images or Sindberg's own words, this book would not have been worth the time.

There were several issues found within the book. Twice, Harmsen writes with authority on a subject without providing evidence. In the first instance, he claims that "There is evidence that Chiang Kai-shek was close to a nervous breakdown" (54) due to Japanese advancement, but he does not provide evidence. That is a bold statement about an international leader without backing up the evidence. Later, he claims that evidence suggests "Sindberg was toying with the idea of getting an education in the United States" (84), yet again does not source the evidence. Then in Chapter 11, Harmsen details the horrible rape of Chinese women and children by Japanese men and then proceeds to say that the men were "behaving like a gang

of naughty schoolboys unexpectedly finding themselves without supervision and able to do as they pleased". His gross, apologist justification of them being merely "naughty schoolboys" for the Japanese raping women and children is unacceptable.

Harmsen tries to show why he refers to Sindberg, whom he affectionately calls "The Dane" throughout the book, by the moniker of "The Schindler of Nanjing" but he, unfortunately, fails. Sindberg got the job at Jiangnan Cement, which serves as the main location for the locals ' savings, not because he was the best or because he was looking to help, but because he was the only one available. And he was not alone. He worked in that factory with a German man, Karl Günther, who was born in China and spoke Chinese. Sindberg may have brought the refugees inside the gates of the factory following the massacre, but it was Gunther's Nazi flags, not the Danish ones, that kept the Japanese at bay. So, compared to Oskar Schindler, it dilutes the real hero and is a device to attract readers to this book by using name recognition.

Overall, for a book that is supposed to be about Sindberg, he is missing from most of the chapters. While it is an interesting story, it felt like I was reading a condensed rehash of Harmsen's other two books, *Shanghai 1937: Stalingrad on the Yangtze* and *Nanjing 1937: Battle for a Doomed City*. For example, Harmsen cited his own work in this book when discussing the events of "Black Saturday" in Chapter 3, showing that he is knowledgeable of the history of the region, but also shows that he had limited content on the main subject, so he filled it with information he has previously written about. So while he fails to argue his main point about Sindberg, if you want to know more about the Japanese invasion of China during the late 1930s, this is a quick book, especially if you like your history with a bit of White Saviorism.

About the Author

Aisha Manus is a part-time mermaid and a full-time cat lady who loves history. She has an MA in US History, a BA in Asian and Pacific history, an AAS in Intelligence, and an AAS in Communication. Aisha is still in school, working on another degree or three. She is a disabled USAF veteran who dreams of being a professor when she grows up.

Book Review: Douglas Brunt's *The Mysterious Case of Rudolf Diesel: Genius, Power, and Deception on the Eve of World War 1*

Clayton Willis

Columbia University

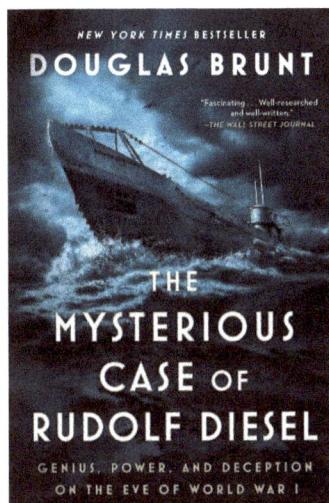

The Mysterious Case of Rudolf Diesel: Genius, Power, and Deception on the Eve of World War 1. Douglas Brunt. New York City, Atria Books, 2023. 384 pp. Hardcover. ISBN: 9781982169909.

Situated in the late 19th century and the years just before the First World War, *The Mysterious Case of Rudolf Diesel* presents a thrilling and memorable story of one of history's greatest inventors and his strange disappearance. German by blood, though raised in Paris for most of his youth, Rudolf Diesel, during the 1870s, set out at an early age, hoping to invent an engine that would revolutionize the world. However, his earth-shattering invention would rattle some of the world's most influential individuals, making his sudden disappearance in September 1913 even more intriguing and leading authors in the modern day to revisit this bewildering vanishing act.

Despite Rudolf Diesel's significant influence on our world, his name is often never associated with his engine, which transformed transportation. Douglas Brunt's ultimate goal with *The Mysterious Case of Rudolf Diesel* is to bring attention to the name Diesel, giving the reader a comprehensive biography of this underappreciated engineer. The biography sets to establish the background of this man's life leading up to his sudden disappearance on board the *SS Dresden* in 1913 and how his life could be interpreted in the handful of speculations behind why and how one of the world's most famous individuals could disappear with little trace. Brunt's years of devotion to this project, requir-

doi: 10.18278/mhc.2.2.8

ing an untold number of hours in archives and museums has created a captivating book that presents enough new evidence regarding Diesel's disappearance to shake the original arguments that have withstood for over a century.

Rudolf Diesel's life began with modest beginnings, being the son of Bavarian immigrants in a less-than-desirable neighborhood in Paris. From a young age, Diesel demonstrated an intense curiosity toward his toys' inner workings, which inspired him to create blueprints of his own contraptions. Once the family was forced to flee Paris for the city of London during the height of the Franco-Prussian War, the teenager began his fascination with engines and how their effects could improve workers' quality of life worldwide. The early chapters of Brunt's book establish the young engineer's deep and obsessive desires that would dictate the rest of his life. Brunt paints an excellent picture of a fiercely intelligent man who aims to help others, where money and prestige only come after the good that a cleaner and more efficient engine could do for society. Despite his disadvantaged upbringing, Diesel cemented himself as one of Europe's best engineers as a young adult, quickly finding himself in positions of power over ice-making manufacturing plants in France and Germany.

Rudolf Diesel's work in the late 19th century led to the development of the Diesel engine, a more efficient and cleaner power source than other engines of its time. A creation of this magnitude set off a chain reaction from both those who either sought to master the diesel engine for themselves or had hoped to destroy the engine before it had disastrous effects on their business. Brunt's writing skills shine bright when intertwining the stories of John D. Rockefeller and Germany's Kaiser Wilhelm, two immensely powerful individuals of the early 20th century who were directly affected by Diesel's new engine. The Kaiser set out to establish a navy that would challenge Britain on a world stage and found that the practicality offered by diesel engines could create a U-boat fleet that could bring the Royal Navy to its knees. However, when German military industrialists attempted to take the engine for themselves, Diesel refused to cooperate, leading to a lawsuit and forever souring the Kaiser's view of the inventor. Rockefeller additionally had antagonistic views of Rudolf Diesel, as Diesel's engine could run on various fuel sources, threatening to topple Rockefeller's monopoly on oil-derived engines. Brunt thoroughly interjects the rising tensions between Diesel and his antagonist throughout the book before 1913, lending readers to question the evidence given on whether these two men had any involvement in the disappearance.

The book's most interesting aspect arises in its third act, following Diesel's disappearance under strange circumstances. Brunt switches gears, writing from a biography to a murder mystery while utilizing all the background information he had presented in the previous chapters to fuel skepticism toward the many theories regarding Diesel's sudden departure. The first of three popular theories about the mysterious disappearance revolves around Diesel accidentally falling from the *SS Dresden* during the night. However, Brunt disregards this theory as unplausible given the circumstances. The second and most widely accepted theory from contemporary journalism from 1913 suggested the vanishing act to be suicide. However, Brunt additionally refutes this theory, as many others have done. The last of the three theories had been hinted at throughout the book, involving murder by either the agents of Rockefeller or the Kaiser. The book had given plenty of evidence throughout Rudolf Diesel's biography, hinting that the likely theory of the three would involve murder. However, Brunt surprises his readers by presenting a fourth option with fewer contradictions than the others.

Douglas Brunt's theory may be the most controversial and potentially unfavorable aspect of *The Mysterious Case of Rudolf Diesel*. Brunt suggests that Diesel may have faked his death and moved to Canada to work under the First Lord of the Admiralty, Winston Churchill, to improve his engine designs for the Royal Navy out of sight of the Kaiser and his agents. This intriguing argument presents evidence from the disappearance that makes more sense than the theories above. However, some readers may need supplementary information to boost this claim, as there may need to be more evidence to persuade readers that the pacificist Rudolf Diesel had suddenly devoted his life to bolstering the world's most powerful navy. However, the limited evidence Brunt delivers makes sense, and additional research by scholars and historians could further support this argument.

The Mysterious Case of Rudolf Diesel provides an excellent life summary of one of the world's most important inventors. Rudolf Diesel may have been pleased to know that Douglas Brunt prioritized giving a thought-out summary of his life. The book belongs with other superb pieces of literature covering the lead-up to one of the world's deadliest conflicts.

About the Author

Clayton Willis recently graduated from Columbia University's MA program in European History, Politics, and Society. His historical interest in 19th and 20th-century European History has led to studies on the First and Second World Wars and the peacekeeping missions of organizations such as the European Union. After graduating, Clayton continues to serve as Senior Advisor for Columbia University's European Union Student Association, an association he was elected Vice President of in 2024. He is currently preparing to begin a PhD in the fall of 2025.

Battlefield Tour: Gettysburg: A Look at A Great American Battlefield

Dr. Robert Young

Professor
Department of History and Military History
American Public University

"I hope this is good ground."

—General George Meade upon his arrival at Gettysburg on July 1, 1863
(from the film *Gettysburg*)

Among America's many national treasures are its Civil War battlefields. None is more compelling or famous than Gettysburg. In early November, my brother and I, both Army veterans who had seen the battlefield during 1990s staff rides, decided to revisit. We also had a personal reason—our great, great, great grandfather, General Samuel Zook, commander of the 3rd Brigade of the Union II Corps' 1st Division, was killed at Gettysburg on Day 2 and has a monument near where he fell.

We also wanted to look over key parts of the battlefield and, in two full days, saw many parts of it. We did not see everything. We decided it would probably take weeks to do so. Some of the highlights are shown on the following pages. Many of the pictures are from

The present-day view of the Day 1 battlefield from the cupola of the Seminary School. Buford's line was extended at the end of the green, from left to right. Source: Author's collection

doi: 10.18278/mhc.2.2.9

The John Reynolds Monument. Reynolds arrived on the battlefield as the Confederate corps of A.P. Hill, and Richard Ewell moved forward in force. Reynolds forces slowed their opponents down but were forced to retreat through Gettysburg to the heights beyond the town. By nightfall, all seven corps of the Union Army had arrived and begun digging in. Reynolds was killed soon after his arrival by a Confederate sharpshooter as he implored his men to move toward the fight. Source: Author's collection

The view from Little Round Top offers a perspective from where the 20th Maine Regiment set up its defense. The incline is roughly 70 degrees at points. Rocks and rough patches are everywhere. On July 2, 1863, trees were scattered across the hill. Imagine the challenge of scaling such a position while trying to maintain any cohesion in your formations as Union rifle fire rained down. Source: Author's collection

key websites because our phones were limited in how much they could capture, and nature has reasserted its dominance 161 years after the battle. Woods and overgrowth obscure what was clear during the battle. Nevertheless, this is an experience anyone interested in history should enjoy.

For those who have not physically visited the battlefield, the 1993 film *Gettysburg* serves as the foundation of their knowledge. Michael Shaara's book *The Killer Angels* covers most aspects of the three-day battle. One aspect it did not cover much was Days 2 and 3 of

the battle on Culp's Hill. Day 1 and the remarkable actions of Buford's cavalry, the incredible defense of the left flank of the Union line on Little Round Top by Joshua Chamberlain's 20th Maine Infantry Regiment, and, of course, Pickett's Charge were where my brother and I spent most of our time.

To understand Day 1 of Gettysburg, one must go into the town of Gettysburg, start at the Seminary School, and go into the "Tower." Here, one can park and walk the town with no difficulty. The Tower was where General John Buford watched the battle that morn-

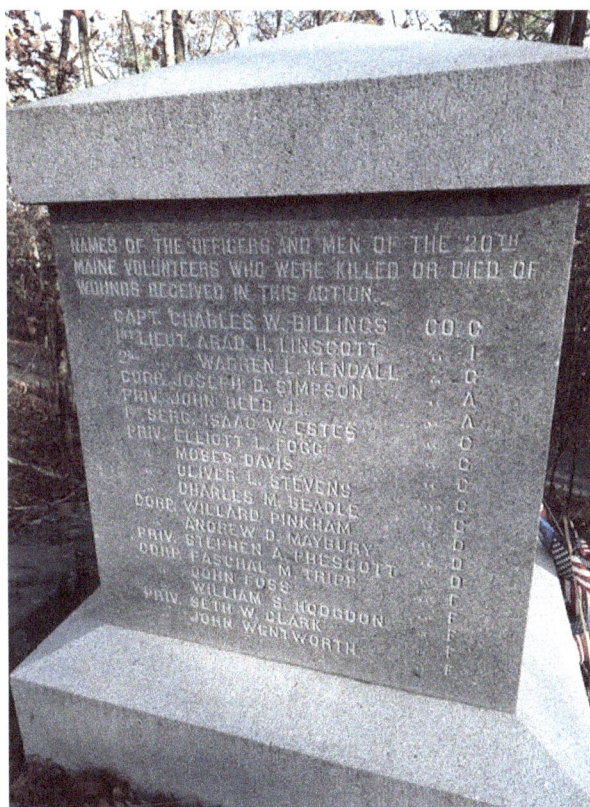

The memorial for the 20th Maine Infantry Regiment stands atop Little Round Top. One might expect a grander monument for such a renowned unit that not only defended their segment of the Union line but also executed perhaps the most famous bayonet charge in American military history. By the end of Day 2, the 20th Maine had approximately 100 of the 400 men left despite starting the day fully fit to fight. Source: Author's collection

The General Gouverneur Warren Monument stands atop Little Round Top. It's a rather simple monument, but its location is awe-inspiring. According to the Park Ranger at Little Round Top, legend has it that the rock on which the Warren Monument is placed is where he stood in alarm, surveying the position and the field below. He sent word to get troops to extend the Union line from this spot. Colonel Strong Vincent's brigade, which included the 20th Maine, arrived just in time. Warren also observed Sickles's corps moving forward, creating a significant gap in the Union line. Source: Author's collection

The author stands at the memorial of his great-great-great-grandfather, General Samuel Zook. General Zook was part of Sickles' Corps and involved in the movement that made the entire Union line vulnerable during the afternoon of Day 2. He was killed as his men engaged with the enemy, doing what many other senior commanders in this war did: acting like a squad leader instead of managing the larger unit. Source: Author's collection

ing of July 1, 1863. The roads leading to what became America's greatest battle are still visible from there.

Buford made his stand across the ground looking over the Chambersburg Pike. He knew it would be a quick stand since even though his 2,500 men were equipped with Spencer repeating rifles, they would only last so long against the divisions of A.P. Hill and General Richard Ewell's Confederate corps. He hoped he could force the Rebels to continue to deploy and redeploy. He was waiting for General John Reynolds and several infantry corps to arrive.

Reynolds arrived, and his men temporarily held Robert E. Lee's Army of Northern Virginia back. Lee's corps under Hill and Ewell were more than double Reynolds's strength, and Union forces retreated through the town to the heights beyond, where Union defenders repulsed repeated Confederate attacks over the next two days. Reynolds played no further part in the battle. He was killed by an enemy sharpshooter soon after his arrival, forever immortalized with this memorial at the approximate spot where he was killed. Though taken so early in the battle, the actions of Buford and Reynolds allowed for the arrival of the rest of the Army of the Potomac that evening, allowing them to take up a very advantageous position.

Another key to this first day was Culp's Hill, which became the far right of the Union line. I will examine this position in detail at the end of this work. One crucial fact of Day 1 was that the Confederates missed their opportunity to seize it before the Union occupied it. Culp's Hill towered over the Baltimore Pike, to the Union line's rear. This

The author stands next to the Longstreet Monument. It serves as a small tribute to a significant leader. Described as "My old war horse" by Lee himself, his time at Gettysburg was marked by controversy, at least from the Confederate viewpoint. He has faced accusations of undermining Lee by not fully backing his decisions. Source: Author's collection

The Confederate perspective on Pickett's Charge involved crossing a mile of open ground to reach the Union line. These magnificent veteran soldiers displayed no hesitation when ordered to advance, fighting until they were driven back while facing artillery fire the whole time, alongside musket and rifle fire as they drew closer.

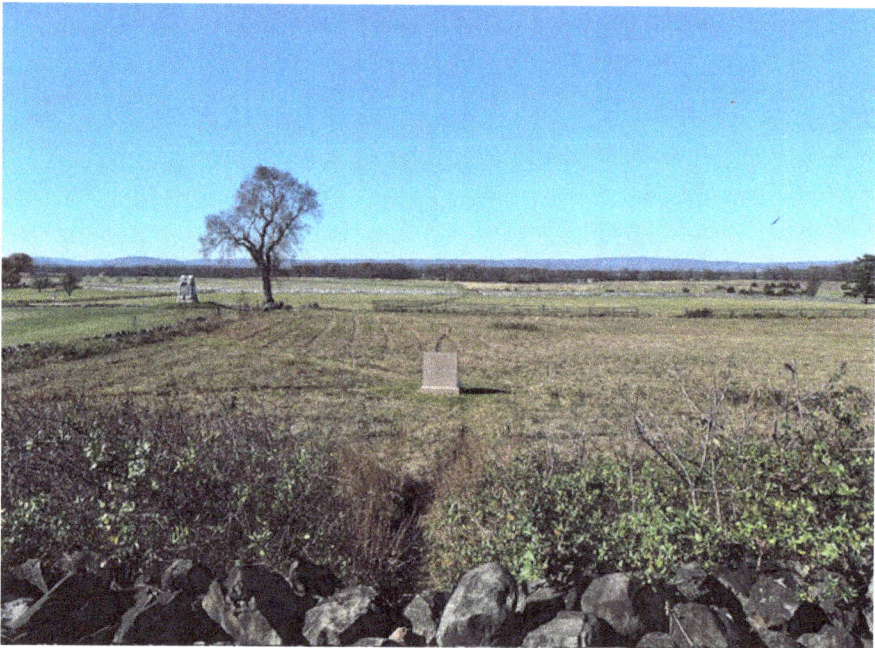

The Union perspective on Pickett's Charge. From behind the rocks, Union infantry could observe the distant tree line as Confederate infantry moved forward. Union artillery also had a clear view and relentlessly targeted the Confederate formations throughout. Source: Author's collection

was the Army of the Potomac's main line of supply and allowed the Army's commander, General George Meade, to move men throughout his line. As Day 1 ended, Culp's Hill was still in Union hands.

Day 2 is most famous for the actions on Little Round Top, and while there were other actions, none garnered the attention of that dogged stand by the 20th Maine. Seeing that horrible terrain amazes me, as the regiment after the regiment of James Longstreet's corps attacked up the hill. Chamberlain's regiment was the last unit on the Union line and decimated the attacking Confederates from their dominating, wooded-high ground. But the 20th Maine was also weakened with every enemy attack. Some of the men were almost out of ammunition, and with yet another attack coming, Colonel Chamberlain

ordered a bayonet charge. Visitors cannot walk this charge, but can see where it went from the various monuments.

There is a monument to General Gouverneur Warren, the Army's chief engineer. He had arranged the defenses on Little Round Top after seeing it undefended. From his position there he also saw the corps of General Daniel Sickles move forward from the main line to an exposed position. It was a foolish move, made worse by Sickles not informing Meade he had done this. A visitor to the battlefield will undoubtedly note I omitted several things—it's just impossible to see everything.

We spent most of our time going over the Day 3 battlefield. That meant Pickett's Charge and Culp's Hill once again, which saw more vicious fighting that third morning. For Pickett's Charge, we were determined to walk

The view from Culp's Hill shows where a Michigan artillery battery was positioned. The ground dips sharply just a few feet from where I stood. Looking ahead, it's clear how any Confederate attack would be very vulnerable and that any Confederate artillery would be ineffective due to the rising ground. Source: Author's collection

General Alexander Webb's Congressional Gold Medal. This gold medal, awarded to Meade and his generals for their actions during this historic battle, was presented to General Webb, who commanded the infantry that repelled Pickett's attack on behalf of the Union League of Philadelphia. Typically, such awards are issued by Congress, but General Ulysses Grant's Vicksburg commanders received theirs for their victory just a day after Meade's triumph at Gettysburg. Perhaps they believed that issuing two sets of medals would diminish their value. Fortunately, Philadelphia's Union League ensured that the leaders of Gettysburg received the recognition they deserved. Source: Author's collection

the route from both perspectives. We started on the Union side and saw the clear lines of fire the Union infantry had when they opened fire, and the multiple artillery batteries all along the Union front had observed shots at Confederate guns along the far tree line and their infantry when they moved out in the open. Then, we walked Pickett's Charge. The long-range guns of the Union artillery exacted an early price, but as the Confederate numbers dwindled and formations began to fall apart, the dangers increased. As Pickett's men closed the distance and passed easy aiming points such as trails and the wooden fence, Union guns firing canister rounds shredded his units even more. We saw where Confederate General Lewis Armistead fell and where his pre-war best friend, Union General Winfield Scott Hancock was wounded. We also saw where Pickett and Longstreet watched the attack, an attack Longstreet never wanted, and one Pickett never recovered from.

We found it ironic that Longstreet's monument was far from the point of attack and hard to find. I was surprised it was in such an obscure place. As a military historian, I know the blame Longstreet received after the war. Along with Jeb Stuart, Lee's cavalry commander, he was roundly criticized for preventing Lee from winning this battle. According to the believers in "The Lost Cause," had Longstreet enthusiastically embraced Lee's plans and decisions, they would have won. A Ranger also did not understand why the monument was so "hidden." That was the word he used. Even more surprising is no Pickett monument exists anywhere. We asked the Park Rangers and

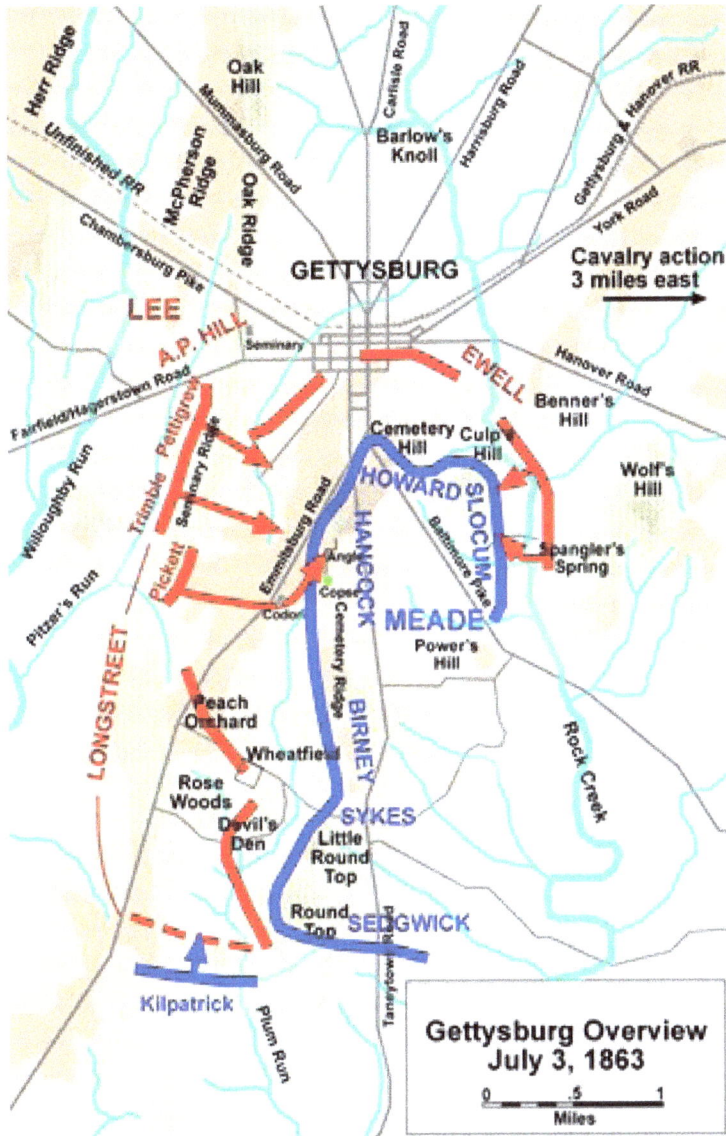

General John Buford's actions on Day 1 saw his 2,500 men initially face two brigades led by Henry Heth. If more Confederate forces arrived from the north, or if Heth advanced his entire division along with any additional reinforcements, Buford would soon be overwhelmed. Reynolds arrived just as the brigades of Devin and Gamble began to retreat. Source: The American Battlefield Trust

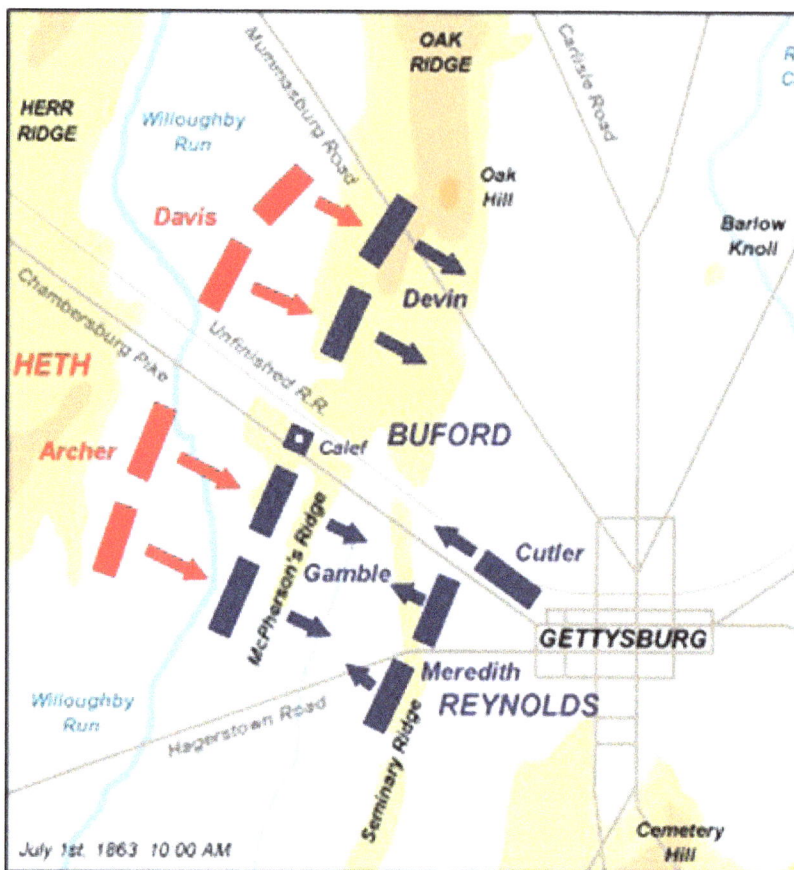

Day 2 at Culp's Hill. The far right of the Union line at Culp's Hill, under the overall command of General James Wadsworth, began to receive Confederate attacks in the early afternoon of July 2. The troops of Confederate General Jones took the forward Union positions. As the day went on, Union reinforcements, including several artillery batteries, strengthened the units on Culp's Hill. They would launch a counterattack just before dawn on July 3, but the Union artillery kept harassing the enemy from their elevated position throughout the night. Source: The American Battlefield Trust

looked at maps. How can the man most famous for this battle not be acknowledged anywhere? Pickett criticized Lee after the war for ordering a hopeless attack. Can this absence and the placement of Longstreet's small monument be a way of protecting Lee? That is a narcissistic way of looking at things, but I am baffled.

Pickett's Charge dominates the talk on Gettysburg and has done so now for 122 years. What of the far right of the Union line, Culp's Hill? I think back to the film *Gettysburg* and the Day 1 engagement as the two overmatched Union corps are retreating through Gettysburg. General Lee was able to see Culp's Hill and undoubtedly recognized its importance. He told his adjutant, Colonel Walter Taylor, to "...find General Ewell and tell him to take that hill if practicable..." Stonewall Jackson had died two months earlier at Chancellorsville. He would not have needed such an order, but had he received it, he would have dashed to Culp's Hill. It became the hook of the Union's fishhook. My brother and I spent more time on Culp's Hill— more than the ground for Pickett's Charge—than anywhere else on the battlefield.

The Confederates did not take Culp's Hill on Day 1. They tried taking it on Day 2 as part of Lee's attacks along the Union front. Union troops, bolstered by parts of the two corps battered the previous day, erected two sets of breastworks, one at the foot of the hill, another further back. The Confederates did manage to take that first set of positions, but throughout the night, Union reinforcements continued to arrive, as did numerous artillery batteries. Throughout the morning of Day 3 Ewell attacked and was repeatedly repulsed. By midday, he abandoned any hopes of taking Culp's Hill.

When driving along the battlefield, we passed Culp's Hill. It is an impressive military position. We drove a thin, windy road to the top, then got out and walked around. It is as tough a position to attack as Little Round Top. The Union guns could devastate any enemy attack, and the ground itself is as uneven as Little Round Top. Because of the numerous cuts and draws Ewell's artillery could not get involved. The failure to take Culp's Hill may have convinced Lee to stake everything on his attack on the Union center with Pickett's Charge. General Alpheus Williams commanded the Union forces on Culp's Hill. He did a

masterful job. There is no monument for him. How many have even heard of him?

Those who fought on Culp's Hill believe they played as crucial a role in winning the battle as did those who fought on Little Round Top or defended Cemetery Ridge against Pickett's Charge. In 1883, at the 20-year anniversary ceremonies at Gettysburg, Asher Lumbard, a member of the 147th Pennsylvania Infantry, stated:

> This contest lasted from 5 until nearly 10 A.M., and at no place along the line was any more determined attempt made (by the enemy) or one that lasted as long. These are facts. You can all attest the correctness of my assertions. And had our division been driven from Culp's Hill, the celebrated charge of Pickett's division would have never been made. To the eye of any man acquainted with military strategy, it is plainly evident that in an attack the enemy could easily advance upon us here. The formation gave them ample opportunity to approach within one hundred yards before our fire could reach them, and once formed, they could, in a short space of time, charge into our lines; and the fact that men were bayoneted immediately outside our temporary works attest to the severity of the struggle and the determination of the enemy in our front.

I tend to agree with him.

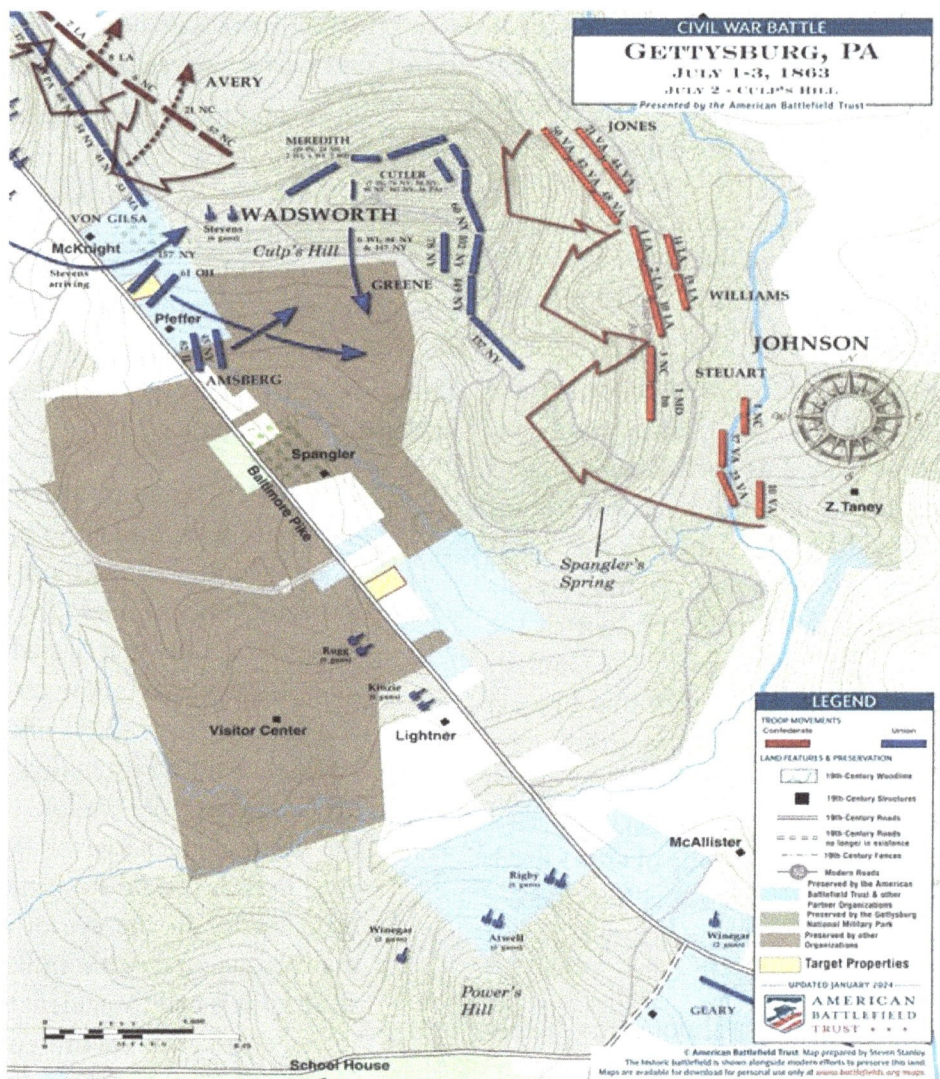

Day 3 at Culp's Hill. Union forces drove the Confederates from the positions they had gained the day before early that morning. Troops from the two Union corps, pushed back by Lee on the first day, reinforced the infantry. Confederate forces from General Richard Ewell's Corps launched several more attacks, but each was repelled, primarily by Union artillery. For most of Day 3, Culp's Hill remained quiet and unassailable. Source: The American Battlefield Trust

Though I have only described and presented parts of the battle, I hope it has given some appreciation of what Gettysburg entails. I would be remiss if I did not mention that Gettysburg, in addition to the battlefield, is home to a wonderful museum at the Welcome/ Visitor Center. In addition to the videos, flags, and mementos, a former Director of the National Civil War Museum in Harrisburg, Pa., volunteers at the Welcome Center once a week. My brother and I were fortunate to meet Dr. Lawrence E. Keener-Farley on that day.

During the Civil War, the Army did not have the current medals and decorations. There was a Congressional Gold Medal. General Ulysses Grant and his chief subordinates were all given that medal for his victory at Vicksburg (the fortress surrendered on July 4, 1863). Gettysburg ended on July 3. Meade and his subordinates did not receive the official Congressional medal. Instead, the Union League of Philadelphia produced twenty-four medals for Meade and his fellow Gettysburg generals. Dr. Keener-Fraley has one of those medals. The one on display at the Museum was given to General Alexander Webb. He commanded the infantry that repelled Pickett. What a great story. I began this with General Meade's statement that he hoped "this is good ground." It was. My next stop is a visit to Chickamauga.

There are some factors that people visiting Gettysburg should consider. One cannot walk this battlefield. Roads intersect the entire area, and the battlefield itself is quite vast. Those who have at least basic knowledge can do it on their own. Just make sure to have a map. If not, consider joining one of the dozens of regularly scheduled tours. For the disabled, the many monuments and fields can be seen from the roads. Walking between those roads and trails is hard for one in a wheelchair or some other impairment. Gettysburg is an excellent place for children, and I saw dozens of students (elementary and middle school age) on field trips. The geography of this battle is incredible, and this is how you build an interest in American history for our youngest. There are websites to help plan a trip, and if you don't know much about the battle, I recommend using a resource like the National Parks Service. https://www.nps.gov/gett/planyourvisit/index.htm/.

Gettysburg National Military Park
1195 Baltimore Pike, Suite 100
Gettysburg, PA 17325-2804
717-334-1124

About the Author

Robert Young earned a Ph.D. in Military History and Modern European Studies from the C.U.N.Y. Graduate Center in 2003, and a master's degree in American History from Brooklyn College in 1994. He is currently a History and Military History professor at American Military University. A veteran of the United States Army, he held various leadership positions in armored and cavalry units.

MILITARY HISTORY CHRONICLES
CALL FOR PAPERS—Winter 2026 CAMPAIGN

The *Military History Chronicles* is soliciting articles, books, and exhibition reviews for its Winter 2026 Campaign.

The theme of MHC is military history exclusively. All historical time periods and geographic regions are welcome, provided they address a topic of historical interest. Book, documentary film, or exhibition reviews should be on recent events, releases, or publications.

Students, alumni, faculty from all academic institutions, and unaffiliated independent scholars are welcome to submit their original work. This includes previously submitted and corrected coursework. In either case, submissions should not have been published elsewhere.

All submissions must adhere to the *Military History Chronicles*' submission guidelines which can be located at: https://saberandscroll. scholasticahq.com/for-authors.

The *Military History Chronicles* reserves the right to reject, without further review, any submissions that do not follow these guidelines or meet our high academic standards.

Any questions should be directed to Jeff B a llard, Editor-in-Chief, the *Military History Chronicles* at: EICatMHC@gmail.com.

DEADLINES

October 1, 2025: Working Title, Abstract (124 words max), and Key-words (8-12).

November 1, 2025: Full Manuscript

This publication is available open access at:
http://www.ipsonet.org/publications/open-access

Thanks to the generosity of the American Public University System

American
Public
APU University

American
Military
AMU University

Policy Studies Organization Resources

The Policy Studies Organization (PSO) is a publisher of academic journals and books, sponsor of conferences, and producer of programs. There are numerous resources available for scholars, including:

Journals

Policy Studies Organization publishes dozens of journals on a range of topics:

Arts & International Affairs
Asian Politics & Policy
China Policy Journal
Digest of Middle East Studies
European Policy Analysis
Latin American Policy
Military History Chronicles
Popular Culture Review
Poverty & Public Policy
Proceedings of the PSO
Review of Policy Research
Risks, Hazards & Crisis in Public Policy
Ritual, Secrecy, & Civil Society
Saber & Scroll Historical Journal
Sculpture, Monuments, and Open Space (formerly Sculpture Review)
Sexuality, Gender & Policy
Security & Intelligence (formerly Global Security & Intelligence Studies)
Space Education and Strategic Applications
International Journal of Criminology
International Journal of Open Educational Resources
Journal on AI Policy and Complex Systems
Journal of Critical Infrastructure Policy
Journal of Indigenous Ways of Being, Knowing, and Doing
Journal of Online Learning Research and Practice

Indian Politics & Polity
Journal of Elder Studies
Policy & Internet
Policy Studies Journal
Policy Studies Yearbook
Politics & Policy
World Affairs
World Food Policy
World Medical & Health Policy
World Water Policy

Conferences

Policy Studies Organization hosts numerous conferences, including the Middle East Dialogue, Space Education and Strategic Applications, International Criminology Conference, Dupont Summit on Science, Technology and Environmental Policy, World Conference on Fraternalism, Freemasonry and History, AI – The Future of Education: Disruptive Teaching and Learning Models, Sport Management and Esport Conference, and the Internet Policy & Politics Conference. Recordings of these talks are available in the PSO Video Library.

Yearbook

The Policy Yearbook contains a detailed international listing of policy scholars with contact information, fields of specialization, research references, and an individual scholar's statements of research interests.

Curriculum Project

The Policy Studies Organization aims to provide resources for educators, policy makers, and community members, to promote the discussion and study of the various policies that affect our local and global society. Our curriculum project organizes PSO articles and other media by easily serachable themes.

For more information on these projects, access videos of past talks, and upcoming events, please visit us at:

ipsonet.org

Related Titles from Westphalia Press

The Limits of Moderation: Jimmy Carter and the Ironies of American Liberalism by Leo P. Ribuffo

The Limits of Moderation: Jimmy Carter and the Ironies of American Liberalism is not a finished product. And yet, even in this unfinished stage, this book is a close and careful history of a short yet transformative period in American political history, when big changes were afoot.

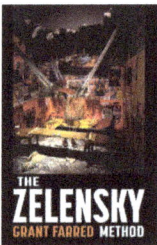

The Zelensky Method by Grant Farred

Locating Russian's war within a global context, The Zelensky Method is unsparing in its critique of those nations, who have refused to condemn Russia's invasion and are doing everything they can to prevent economic sanctions from being imposed on the Kremlin.

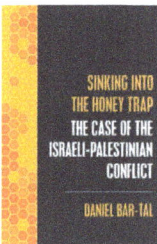

Sinking into the Honey Trap: The Case of the Israeli-Palestinian Conflict by Daniel Bar-Tal, Barbara Doron, Translator

Sinking into the Honey Trap by Daniel Bar-Tal discusses how politics led Israel to advancing the occupation, and of the deterioration of democracy and morality that accelerates the growth of an authoritarian regime with nationalism and religiosity.

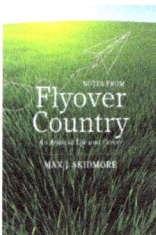

Notes From Flyover Country: An Atypical Life & Career by Max J. Skidmore

In this remarkable book, Skidmore discusses his "atypical life and career," and includes work from his long life in academe. Essays deal with the principles and creation of constitutions, anti-government attitudes, the influence of language usage on politics, and church-state relations.

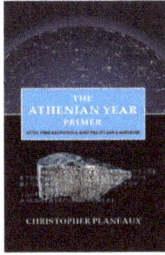

The Athenian Year Primer: Attic Time-Reckoning and the Julian Calendar
by Christopher Planeaux

The ability to translate ancient Athenian calendar references into precise Julian-Gregorian dates will not only assist Ancient Historians and Classicists to date numerous historical events with much greater accuracy but also aid epigraphists in the restorations of numerous Attic inscriptions.

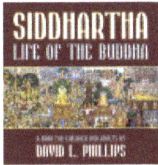

Siddhartha: Life of the Buddha
by David L. Phillips,
contributions by Venerable Sitagu Sayadaw

Siddhartha: Life of the Buddha is an illustrated story for adults and children about the Buddha's birth, enlightenment and work for social justice. It includes illustrations from Pagan, Burma which are provided by Rev. Sitagu Sayadaw.

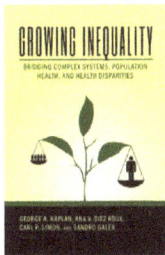

Growing Inequality: Bridging Complex Systems, Population Health, and Health Disparities
Editors: George A. Kaplan, Ana V. Diez Roux, Carl P. Simon, and Sandro Galea

Why is America's health is poorer than the health of other wealthy countries and why health inequities persist despite our efforts? In this book, researchers report on groundbreaking insights to simulate how these determinants come together to produce levels of population health and disparities and test new solutions.

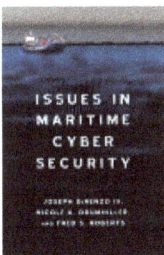

Issues in Maritime Cyber Security
Edited by Dr. Joe DiRenzo III, Dr. Nicole K. Drumhiller, and Dr. Fred S. Roberts

The complexity of making MTS safe from cyber attack is daunting and the need for all stakeholders in both government (at all levels) and private industry to be involved in cyber security is more significant than ever as the use of the MTS continues to grow.

Female Emancipation and Masonic Membership: An Essential Collection
By Guillermo De Los Reyes Heredia

Female Emancipation and Masonic Membership: An Essential Combination is a collection of essays on Freemasonry and gender that promotes a transatlantic discussion of the study of the history of women and Freemasonry and their contribution in different countries.

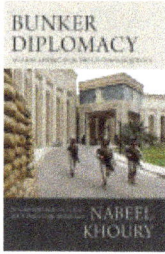

Bunker Diplomacy: An Arab-American in the U.S. Foreign Service
by Nabeel Khoury

After twenty-five years in the Foreign Service, Dr. Nabeel A. Khoury retired from the U.S. Department of State in 2013 with the rank of Minister Counselor. In his last overseas posting, Khoury served as deputy chief of mission at the U.S. embassy in Yemen (2004-2007).

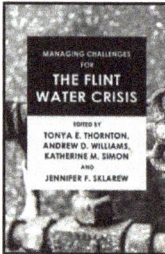

Managing Challenges for the Flint Water Crisis
Edited by Toyna E. Thornton, Andrew D. Williams, Katherine M. Simon, Jennifer F. Sklarew

This edited volume examines several public management and intergovernmental failures, with particular attention on social, political, and financial impacts. Understanding disaster meaning, even causality, is essential to the problem-solving process.

User-Centric Design
by Dr. Diane Stottlemyer

User-centric strategy can improve by using tools to manage performance using specific techniques. User-centric design is based on and centered around the users. They are an essential part of the design process and should have a say in what they want and need from the application based on behavior and performance.

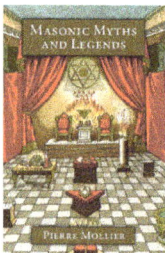

Masonic Myths and Legends
by Pierre Mollier

Freemasonry is one of the few organizations whose teaching method is still based on symbols. It presents these symbols by inserting them into legends that are told to its members in initiation ceremonies. But its history itself has also given rise to a whole mythology.

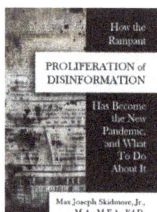

How the Rampant Proliferation of Disinformation has Become the New Pandemic by Max Joseph Skidmore Jr.

This work examines the causes of the overwhelming tidal wave of fake news, misinformation, disinformation, and propaganda, and the increase in information illiteracy and mistrust in higher education and traditional, vetted news outlets that make fact-checking a priority

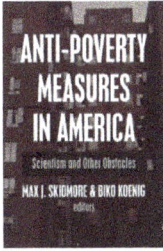

Anti-Poverty Measures in America: Scientism and Other Obstacles
Editors, Max J. Skidmore and Biko Koenig

Anti-Poverty Measures in America brings together a remarkable collection of essays dealing with the inhibiting effects of scientism, an over-dependence on scientific methodology that is prevalent in the social sciences, and other obstacles to anti-poverty legislation.

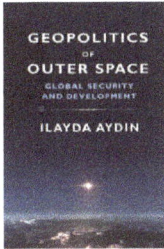

Geopolitics of Outer Space: Global Security and Development
by Ilayda Aydin

A desire for increased security and rapid development is driving nation-states to engage in an intensifying competition for the unique assets of space. This book analyses the Chinese-American space discourse from the lenses of international relations theory, history and political psychology to explore these questions.

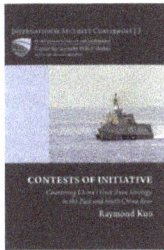

Contests of Initiative: Countering China's Gray Zone Strategy in the East and South China Seas
by Dr. Raymond Kuo

China is engaged in a widespread assertion of sovereignty in the South and East China Seas. It employs a "gray zone" strategy: using coercive but sub-conventional military power to drive off challengers and prevent escalation, while simultaneously seizing territory and asserting maritime control.

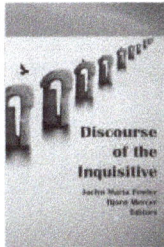

Discourse of the Inquisitive
Editors: Jaclyn Maria Fowler and Bjorn Mercer

Good communication skills are necessary for articulating learning, especially in online classrooms. It is often through writing that learners demonstrate their ability to analyze and synthesize the new concepts presented in the classroom.

westphaliapress.org

www.ingramcontent.com/pod-product-compliance
Lightning Source LLC
Chambersburg PA
CBHW081427090426
42740CB00017B/3207